AF748844

Social Media and Law Enforcement Practice in Poland

This book explores the role of social media in the daily practice of Polish criminal justice and how social media is, in turn, reshaping this practice. Based on empirical research, it confronts common beliefs about how police officers, prosecutors, and judges use social media in their work. Readers will find answers to the following questions: Which social media platforms are popular among law enforcement officers in Poland? How do the police use social media to investigate and prosecute crimes? What are the strategies for using social media to communicate with the community? What strategies are most successful?

The findings in this book challenge some popular beliefs and theories about social media in criminal justice. As the first book to explore the use of social media in criminal justice outside of English-speaking countries, this collection of academic research will be of interest to academics focusing on criminology, criminal justice, and policing and will be useful to police leaders and officers, police social media administrators, prosecutors, and judges, who may be inspired by the research to implement new successful and more effective practices.

Paweł Waszkiewicz is a university professor in the Department of Criminalistics at the Faculty of Law and Administration of the University of Warsaw. He has been a lecturer and visiting professor at the University of Ottawa, Rutgers University, University College London, Universidad de Alicante, Universidad de Malaga, and Teesside University, among others. He has led and co-led research on crime prevention, video surveillance, biometrics, operational and detection work, homicide investigation, surveillance methods, and out of court conflict resolution funded by Polish (Ministry of Science and Higher Education, National Science Center, University of Warsaw) and foreign (European Commission, Södertörn University, Foundation for Baltic and East European Studies) grants.

Paweł Waszkiewicz is the author and coauthor of dozens of scientific publications and more than a hundred conference presentations. He is an advocate of evidence-based activities, transparency, and open-access policies. Most of his publications are freely available on his researchgate.net and academia.edu profiles.

Self-appointed president of the Warsaw fan club of the TV series The Wire. In love with surfing without reciprocation.

Routledge Studies in Crime, Media and Culture

Routledge Studies in Crime, Media and Culture offers the very best in research that seeks to understand crime through the context of culture, cultural processes and media.

The series welcomes monographs and edited volumes from across the globe, and across a variety of disciplines. Books will offer fresh insights on a range of topics, including news reporting of crime; moral panics and trial by media; media and the police; crime in film; crime in fiction; crime in TV; crime and music; 'reality' crime shows; the impact of new media including mobile, Internet and digital technologies, and social networking sites; the ways media portrayals of crime influence government policy and lawmaking; the theoretical, conceptual and methodological underpinnings of cultural criminology.

Books in the series will be essential reading for those researching and studying criminology, media studies, cultural studies and sociology.

An Epistemology of Criminological Cinema
David Grčki and Rafe McGregor

The American City in Crime Films
Criminology and the Cinematic City
Andrew J. Baranauskas

Video Games, Crime and Control
Playing Cops and Robbers
Edited by Jonathan A. Grubb and Kevin F. Steinmetz

Social Media and Law Enforcement Practice in Poland
Insights into Practice Outside Anglophone Countries
Edited by Paweł Waszkiewicz

Social Media and Law Enforcement Practice in Poland

Insights into Practice Outside Anglophone Countries

Edited by Paweł Waszkiewicz

Routledge
Taylor & Francis Group
NEW YORK AND LONDON

First published 2024
by Routledge
605 Third Avenue, New York, NY 10158

and by Routledge
4 Park Square, Milton Park, Abingdon, Oxon, OX14 4RN

Routledge is an imprint of the Taylor & Francis Group, an informa business

© 2024 selection and editorial matter, Paweł Waszkiewicz; individual chapters, the contributors

The right of Paweł Waszkiewicz to be identified as the author of the editorial material, and of the authors for their individual chapters, has been asserted in accordance with sections 77 and 78 of the Copyright, Designs and Patents Act 1988.

The Open Access version of this book, available at www.taylorfrancis.com, has been made available under a Creative Commons Attribution-NonCommercial (CC-BY-NC) 4.0 International license.

Any third party material in this book is not included in the OA Creative Commons license, unless indicated otherwise in a credit line to the material. Please direct any permissions enquiries to the original rightsholder.

The costs of the Open Access publication were covered by the University of Warsaw under the Excellence Initiative Research University Action I.2.4 Supporting Open Access Publications.

Trademark notice: Product or corporate names may be trademarks or registered trademarks, and are used only for identification and explanation without intent to infringe.

This book is a result of the research project no 2018/31/B/HS5/01876 funded by the Polish National Science Centre entitled ‘Social Media in Law Enforcement Practice’.

ISBN: 978-1-032-68018-7 (hbk)
ISBN: 978-1-032-68021-7 (pbk)
ISBN: 978-1-032-68019-4 (ebk)

DOI: 10.4324/9781032680194

Typeset in Times New Roman
by Apex CoVantage, LLC

Contents

Contributor biographies

Piotr Lewulis is an assistant professor in the Department of Criminalistics at the Faculty of Law and Administration, University of Warsaw. He also leads the Postgraduate Studies in Evidence Law and Crime Science at the University's Center for Judicial Sciences. He has international academic experience as an affiliate academic at University College London and as a research intern at Rutgers University. He has made significant contributions to nationally and internationally funded research projects on various topics, including homicide investigation methods, the competency of court experts, counter-terrorism, and the role of digital evidence in legal proceedings.

An advocate for integrating theoretical knowledge with practical application, Piotr Lewulis is committed to academic teaching and research activities. He has authored numerous publications and presented at various conferences, emphasizing the importance of digital evidence in the legal landscape. In addition to his academic achievements, he is an enthusiastic rock climber and a former member of the University of Warsaw snowboard team.

Stanisław Rabczuk is a PhD candidate in the Department of Criminalistics at the Faculty of Law and Administration, University of Warsaw. He gained his research experience by participating in the project on the use of social media by law enforcement agencies, founded by the Polish National Science Center. His research interests evolve around the use of modern technologies by law enforcement agencies and cross-border access to electronic evidence. A member of the Warsaw Bar Association, he practices law and teaches criminalistics at the University of Warsaw. He also runs courses on Postgraduate Studies in Evidence Law and Crime Science at the University's Center for Judicial Sciences, the Open University of Warsaw University. He is a third-class glider pilot with a private interest in aviation.

Błażej Stromczyński is PhD candidate in the Department of Criminalistics at the Faculty of Law and Administration, University of Warsaw. He participated in research projects on homicide investigations and social media use of law enforcement. The lecturer on Postgraduate Studies in Evidence Law and Crime Science at the University's Center for Judicial Sciences and the Open University at the University of Warsaw. He uses his academic knowledge in practice while professionally conducting internal investigations on fraud, corruption, and other misconduct.

Magdalena Tomaszewska-Michalak is an assistant professor in the Department of Internal Security at the Faculty of Political Science and International Studies at the University of Warsaw. She participated in many research projects regarding biometrics, homicide investigation, the use of social media by law enforcement agencies, and Chemical, Biological, Radiological, and Nuclear (CBRN) safety.

She is the author and co-author of several scientific publications. She participated in national and international conferences, where she especially pointed out the importance of legal and social aspects of introducing new technologies.

Krzysztof Worek is a PhD candidate in the Department of Criminalistics, Faculty of Law and Administration, University of Warsaw. A lawyer and psychologist, he is a lecturer in postgraduate studies in evidence law and crime science at the University's Center for Judicial Sciences and the Open University of Warsaw University. He has participated in various research projects funded by the National Science Center on social media in law enforcement work and delinquency and antisocial behaviors of juveniles. Apart from leading a project on hate crimes in social media (funded by the Minister of Education and Science), he is the author of numerous scientific publications and national and international conference papers.

1 Social media and criminal justice practice outside the Anglophone countries

Paweł Waszkiewicz

Introduction

Social media plays an increasingly significant role not only in the lives of billions of users but also in the daily practices of criminal justice. However, this topic has not been adequately surveyed. Most of the published literature is theoretical or based on anecdotal evidence. Empirical research on this topic is limited and only covers a small portion of the relevant areas. In their literature review, Walsh and O'Connor (2019) acknowledged this lack and signaled the need for further research. Additionally, existing studies have primarily described the reality of English-speaking countries, particularly the United States. This may limit the translation of their findings to the reality of other countries with different social, cultural, and legal backgrounds and criminal justice systems.

This book aims to address this gap in the existing literature by presenting the results of a mixed-methods research project on social media in criminal justice practice. The project was conducted in Poland – that is, outside the Anglophone countries – between 2019 and 2022.

This chapter provides the theoretical background of the project, states its main objective, and explains the formulated hypotheses. The research methods used in the project are presented and discussed. Additionally, as the project was conducted in Poland, the chapter briefly presents the Polish model of criminal justice.

Social media, law enforcement, criminal justice

Social media has a longer history than one might think: the first successful projects, such as classmates.com and theglobe.com, emerged in the mid-1990s. The years between 2004 and 2011 saw the founding of platforms that are now well-known and widely used around the world, including Facebook (2004), YouTube (2005), Twitter (2006), Tumblr (2007), Instagram (2010), and Snapchat (2011). Facebook and other social media platforms were set up with the primary goal of facilitating communication and entertainment; however,

DOI: 10.4324/9781032680194-1
This chapter has been made available under a CC-BY-NC 4.0 license.

social media quickly became an omnipresent phenomenon. The number of active users and the time spent using social media are objective indicators of its impact. As of December 2023, there were 4.95 billion social media users, accounting for over 60% of the world's population (Statista, 2023a). Facebook, which has remained the most popular platform for the past 15 years, had 3 billion monthly active users in the third quarter of 2023 (Statista, 2023b). On average, users spend 2 hours and 31 minutes on social media daily. Additionally, social media makes up more than one-third of the total time spent using the Internet (Kemp, 2023). One consequence of more time being spent on social media is the shift from traditional to virtual methods of communication and opinion sharing. The above data confirm the significant role of social media in the lives of global users in terms of quantity; however, the qualitative dimension involves the transfer of a series of strictly "analog" interactions to the online world. Social media platforms are not limited to simple communication through messages, photos, and links.

The impact of social media has been the subject of various analyses and studies. Literature on the correlation between social media and problems such as cyberbullying and sexting has also described the phenomenon of "Facebook depression" (O'Keeffe & Clarke-Pearson, 2011). Another potential side effect of using social media is the fear of real-world interactions, which can ultimately lead to withdrawal from them (Rosen, 2007). Social media can even have an impact on the social and political lives of individuals and groups who do not use these platforms; for example, it has been known to play a role in political revolutions and other significant changes. The explosion and development of the so-called Arab Spring (2010–11) have commonly been associated with the activities of supporters of change on social media, mainly Facebook and Twitter (Stepanova, 2011; Wolfsfeld et al., 2013). A heterogeneous group of social protests in geographically and culturally diverse countries, including Moldova in 2009, Iran in 2009–10, Tunisia in 2010–11, Egypt in 2011, and Ukraine in 2013–14, was even labeled as "Twitter Revolutions" (Esfandiari, 2010; Duncombe, 2011). The unexpected outcomes of democratic elections and referenda in 2016 and 2017 on both sides of the Atlantic have been attributed to the influence of social media (Olson, 2016; Allcott & Gentzkow, 2017); this was partially confirmed by the Cambridge Analytica/Facebook scandal (Hern, 2018).

Nowadays, social media is a distinct ecosystem and a significant part of offline reality; people spend longer on social media than on eating or socializing outside the network (Asano, 2017). This applies not only to law-abiding citizens but also to criminals and law enforcement personnel. In fact, an increasing number of law enforcement agencies now have official social media accounts, for example on Facebook or Twitter. Out of the approximately 65 million fan pages belonging to various institutions, companies, and individuals, thousands are developed and managed by law enforcement agencies. At the time of writing, the Federal Bureau of Investigation (FBI) has 2.9 million fans on

Facebook, while the New York City Police Department (NYPD) has 948,000 and the London Metropolitan Police has 367,000. The Facebook profile of the Polish Police has 444,000 fans, and the Regional Police Department, with its headquarters in Poznań, has 53,000.

Law enforcement agencies may use social media to obtain information during investigations, for example through Open-Source Intelligence (OSINT), collecting evidence, and disseminating important information. The literature defines nine specific areas in which law enforcement agencies can utilize social media, including OSINT: Social Media as a Source of Criminal Information, Having a Voice on Social Media, Social Media to Push Information, Social Media to Leverage the Wisdom of the Crowd, Social Media to Interact with the Public, Social Media for Community Policing, Social Media to Show the Human Side of Policing, Social Media to Support Police IT Infrastructure, and Social Media for Efficient Policing (Denef et al. 2012, p. 12). This shows the range of possibilities associated with social media from a law enforcement perspective. Properly applied, these possibilities can bring numerous benefits to both police work and public relations, indirectly affecting law enforcement agencies' work and its consequences. According to Stevens (2010) and Cohen (2010), the authors dealing with this subject are unanimous on the benefits of social media; however, comprehensive research is lacking.

The number of publications discussing the potential of social media is increasing; however, empirical research on this topic is limited and only covers a small portion of the relevant areas. Wall and Williams (2013) concentrated on policing cybercrime through social media. In a special issue of the journal *Policing and Society*, they identified an important intersection of cybercrime and social media, but despite a rich theoretical and anecdotal background, they noted a lack of empirical research data. They stated:

> There is a pressing need to continue research on the themes touched upon in this collection of papers, not only to complement the recent zeal in policy and operational domains but to also advance the criminological discipline so that it remains relevant to emerging "digital societies and publics."
>
> (Wall & Williams, 2013, p. 412)

The monograph *Social Media Strategy in Policing*, edited by Akhgar et al. (2019), presents 13 chapters that cover various theoretical frameworks and practical methods. However, only one chapter, by Nitsch and Allertseder, describes a case study.

Only a few empirical studies have investigated the use of social media by law enforcement agencies. These are typically case studies, for example, on the use of selected social media for communication with local communities (Dai et al., 2017). Denef et al. (2013) studied the use of Twitter by the London police in connection with the 2011 riots, while Meijer and Thaens (2013) compared the publication strategies of three large police units. Altunbas (2013) conducted

12 interviews with social media officers and media relations officers from nine city police departments in the Dallas–Worth area. He also observed the social media activity of those police departments for three months. In his influential work, Schneider (2016) examined the utilization of social media by police in Canada through a media logic framework; his empirical data were derived from four case studies. There are even smaller bodies of literature on the use of social media by other actors in the criminal justice system, such as judges, and on the use of social media evidence during trials.

In their extensive review of the literature on social media and policing, Walsh and O'Connor (2019) concluded that further empirical work was needed: "studies of social media surveillance, in particular, are generally theoretical and speculative, accentuating its potentialities, both good and bad, or drawing on exemplary and idiosyncratic cases" (pp. 8–9). Hu and Lovrich (2020) analyzed electronic community-oriented policing, noting the lack of empirical research in this area. They stated that "police use of social media thus far has not been adequately studied in the criminal justice discipline" (p. 29). Despite the apparent abundance of published works in the years since the call for more research by Wall and Williams in 2013, not much has changed in this area.

Research on social media in criminal justice has been conducted primarily in English-speaking countries, leading to a bias in the published studies. Exceptions to this trend have included studies conducted in Scandinavia (Rønn et al., 2021), Germany (Jungblut et al., 2022), and Poland (Waszkiewicz, 2021, 2022), but there is still a need for more diverse research in this area.

A comparative summary of criminal justice systems in English-speaking countries and Poland

Most research on criminal justice is conducted in English-speaking countries. This is especially true for social media-related projects published in reputable international journals or monographs. It is important to consider the location of the research, as social, cultural, and legal aspects may vary. Most English-speaking countries follow the common law system, while the rest of the world generally follows systems similar to civil law, including criminal law. Additionally, there are differences in the organization of criminal proceedings, with common law countries using an adversarial process and the majority of other countries using inquisitorial or mixed models. Regarding social media, this mainly impacts the ability of law enforcement agencies to collect and present evidence. Additionally, differences in the organization of law enforcement agencies can affect the results of studies conducted in English-speaking countries compared to elsewhere. This is particularly evident in the United States, where most research is conducted and subsequently published: law enforcement there is highly decentralized, resulting in variations not only between states but also within them. Before presenting the criminal justice system in Poland, it is important to highlight these differences.

The Polish criminal law system is considered to be mixed, with a significant prevalence of inquisitorial elements. In 2013, some adversarial elements were introduced, which became effective in July 2015. One reason for this was the limitation of the evidentiary proceedings activity of parties in the non-adversarial model (Jasiński, 2015). However, these changes were quickly reversed. The criminal procedure is two-instance. Poland has three levels of common courts: 318 local courts (*sądy rejonowe*), 47 district courts (*sądy okręgowe*), and 11 appellate courts (*sądy apelacyjne*). Local courts hear misdemeanor and some felony cases in the first instance; district courts hear appeals from local court decisions and more serious felony cases, such as murder, in the first instance. Appellate courts only hear appeals from cases heard by district courts. To become a judge in Poland, one must have a law degree, pass a state examination preceded by a three-year apprenticeship, and complete one year of training. Judges are appointed by the president of Poland; there are nearly 10,000 of them, of whom less than 30% (2,864) preside over criminal cases in the penal departments of each common court (Gębarska & Sobocińska, 2022).

Law enforcement in Poland is centralized, with four organizational levels in the Polish police: the National Police Headquarters (Komenda Główna Policji), 17 Regional Police Departments (*komendy wojewódzkie policji*), 65 City Police Departments (for larger cities), and 271 County Police Departments. This structure corresponds to the administrative division of Poland, which has 16 regions (*województwa*), 314 counties (*powiaty*), and 66 cities with county rights. The Polish police force, which comprises around 100,000 officers, is overseen by a Chief of Police appointed by the prime minister upon recommendation from the Ministry of Internal Affairs. The chiefs of the Regional Police Departments are appointed by the Ministry of Internal Affairs based on the proposal of the Chief of Police and the opinion of the provincial governor. The chiefs of both urban and rural police stations are appointed by the chiefs of regional police stations, with the approval of local government authorities.

The public prosecutor's office in Poland is even more centralized; it is led by the General Public Prosecutor, who since 2016 has been the Minister of Justice. The Ministry of Justice appoints both the National Public Prosecutor and the heads of each prosecutor's office. The organization of the public prosecutor's office follows a geographical structure similar to that of the police and almost identical to that of the courts: there are 11 regional prosecutors' offices (*prokuratura regionalna*), 46 district prosecutors' offices (*prokuratura okręgowa*), and 342 local prosecutors' offices (*prokuratura rejonowa*). To become a prosecutor in Poland, one must have a law degree, pass a state examination (preceded by a three-year apprenticeship), and complete one year of training. Poland has a higher number of prosecutors than many other European countries, with almost 6,000 compared to Germany's approximately 5,000, even though Poland has less than half of Germany's population. This discrepancy is a result of the additional duties that prosecutors in Poland have: they are responsible for conducting criminal investigations and delegating some tasks to the police as part of law enforcement. Additionally, prosecutors are part of the Polish inquisitorial criminal justice system, as they bring charges, prosecute, and act as a party in court proceedings. They conduct investigations independently and have a complete picture of investigative and judicial activities. In our study, we classify both police officers and prosecutors as law enforcement officials.

The *Social Media in Law Enforcement Practice* project

The objective of the *Social Media in Law Enforcement Practice* project, funded by the Polish National Center of Science, was to analyze the scale and methods of social media use by law enforcement agencies, as well as the impact of social media on the functioning of these institutions.

The main hypothesis of the project was that law enforcement agencies underutilize social media (H1), and when they do use it, it is primarily to support ongoing investigations. This was based on preliminary research conducted in the United States and Poland, as well as a preliminary pilot among Polish law enforcement officers. The second exploratory hypothesis was that the use of social media by law enforcement agencies has various effects on their functioning (H2). While this hypothesis seemed obvious at the functional level, the nature and extent of these effects needed to be verified. According to Schneider (2016), there are possible types, but empirical research has not yet confirmed this.

The main hypothesis at the explanatory level was that law enforcement personnel have limited knowledge about the use of social media in their work (H3). This was based on research findings that confirmed the low level of knowledge about the technological potential for the use of social media by law enforcement officers, as well as on the Red Queen Hypothesis, which posits a constant arms race between criminals and those fighting crime. Law enforcement agencies are typically reactive rather than proactive, often responding to crimes after they have been committed rather than anticipating them. This led to the development of the fourth explanatory hypothesis – that there are no laws, codes of conduct, or best practices regulating the use of social media by law enforcement agencies (H4). These four assumptions led to two further specific hypotheses. First, the use of social media by law enforcement agencies will vary depending on the age of the investigators and the popularity of social media in the respective community (H5). Second, the use of social media by law enforcement agencies depends on the existence of legal acts, codes of conduct, and good practices that regulate its use (H6). The preliminary research and consultations conducted prior to the project's preparation confirmed the validity of the proposed hypotheses: law enforcement agencies rarely use social media in their work, and when they do, it is often done in an ad hoc manner without an organizational framework.

To mitigate bias, we employed three types of triangulation (Webb et al., 1966; Campbell & Fiske, 1959): data, researcher, and research method (Denzin, 2009). To ensure data triangulation, research was conducted in various geographical locations (cities) and different law enforcement agencies. Police forces and prosecutors' offices were selected for the research as they play the most significant roles among law enforcement agencies in Poland. Triangulation of researchers was achieved by including individuals with diverse professional and life experiences in the research team. The study was conducted over a period of 36 months (2019–22) by three independent groups, comprising a total of 27 individuals: Katarzyna Bayer, Jan Bitner, Anna Chabiera, Ewa Chmiel, Katarzyna Chruścińska, Marta Czekalska, Szymon Czerwiński, Filip Dąbrowski, Jacek Dembiński, Hubert Dębniak, Barbara Domańska, Marta Gliszczyńska, Adam Goliasz, Aleksandra Jędrzejak, Paulina Kargul, Miłosz Klotz, Martyna Korkus, Kinga Krawczyk, Piotr Lewulis, Jakub Nadolny, Agnieszka Nawara, Stanisław Rabczuk, Karolina Skraba, Błażej Stromczyński, Ignacy Strzałkowski, Magdalena Tomaszewska-Michalak, and Krzysztof Worek. The project's coordinating principal investigator was Paweł Waszkiewicz. Triangulation of research methods was achieved by using both quantitative and qualitative approaches. The study employed various methods, including questionnaire interviews with police officers and prosecutors, analysis of court files and decisions, observation of social media law enforcement activities, and analysis of Facebook Insights for Polish police accounts. Some methods, such as analyzing court files and Facebook Insights, have not yet been used by other academics to explore criminal justice experiences with social media. Surveys of court files are seldom conducted due to formal limitations and the time-consuming nature of this method. Similarly, interviews with active police officers and prosecutors are not commonly employed as a research method due to the specific culture of law enforcement.

We have tried to place the results of our research within the framework of criminological theories. To explain the findings, we considered several theories, including Routine Activity Theory, Social Learning Theory, Rational Choice Theory, and Situational Crime Prevention. Each chapter discusses the findings; the final chapter integrates the results of the triangulated research to determine the most appropriate theoretical framework.

Book layout

This book examines the use of social media by law enforcement agencies and the judiciary in Poland. It analyzes the extent and methods of social media usage by law enforcement agencies and their officers, as well as the impact of social media on the functioning of these institutions and individual officers. Its objective is to gain a better understanding of the relationship between social media and criminal justice by focusing on the behavior of various criminal justice agents. Each chapter centers on a specific aspect of criminal justice and its interaction with social media; each is intended to be both a self-contained entity and part of a book presenting the results of the research project *Social Media in Law Enforcement Practice*.

In Chapter 2, "The Online Frontier: Social Media Use by Law Enforcement Personnel in Poland," Stanisław Rabczuk describes prosecutors' and police officers' use of social media to achieve the goals of the criminal justice system. Our hypothesis was that there would be a significant correlation between age, gender, and private use of social media, and the use of social media at work. We confirmed some correlations but were surprised to find that others were not significant.

To our knowledge, no previous researcher has ever had access to law enforcement social media administrative data, such as Facebook Insights. Access to administrative data for Facebook, the most popular social media platform in Polish society and among law enforcement agents, enabled us to achieve several goals. First, we could study and describe the daily practices of site administrators. Second, we could analyze the reactions of their offline audience – the only way to assess whether the agency's objectives were achieved. We began collecting Facebook Insights prior to the COVID-19 pandemic, which enabled us to compare the role of social media in policing before and during the pandemic. In response to a Freedom of Information Act request, we received data from 13 out of 17 Regional Police Department profiles. Two chapters present analysis of this data. Chapter 3, "Paw Patrol? How Polish Police Are Using Animal Images and Funny Content on Social Media," by Magdalena Tomaszewska-Michalak, analyzes the strategy of attracting followers on social media by posting funny content and animal pictures. Chapter 4, "We Are Still Here – Police Activity on Social Media During the COVID-19 Pandemic," by Błażej Stromczyński, also discusses this topic. Police activity on social media during the COVID-19 pandemic is compared by analyzing profiles and content published by Regional Police Departments on Facebook before (March 2018 to January 2020) and during the pandemic (January 2020 to March 2021). The study aims to investigate changes in police communication strategies during the pandemic.

To accurately describe the phenomenon under study, we analyzed court records to determine the frequency, timing, reasons, and impact of social media usage in the criminal justice process. We also conducted a detailed analysis of hate crimes. Chapters 5 and 6 present both quantitative and qualitative analyses of court files. In Chapter 5, "Social Media Evidence in Criminal Proceedings," Paweł Waszkiewicz and Krzysztof Worek present the results of a quantitative study of court files, analyzing the sources of evidence, how it is secured, and its later use during trial. The study finds that social media is increasingly being used as a source of evidence in criminal cases. A comparison between cases with social media evidence and those without is presented to test the hypothesis regarding the impact of social media evidence. Chapter 6, by Piotr Lewulis,

"Detecting Online Offenders: A Case Study of Social Media Hate Speech Investigations," describes the strategies used by Polish law enforcement to identify perpetrators of social media crimes; it also assesses their motives and perceptions.

The final chapter summarizes the project's findings, evaluates the appropriateness of the selected theoretical frameworks, and suggests policy implications.

References

Akhgar, B., Bayerl, P. S., & Leventakis, G. (Eds.). (2019). *Social media strategy in policing*. Springer.

Allcott, H., & Gentzkow, H. (2017). Social media and fake news in the 2016 election. *National Bureau of Economic Research*, w23089. https://doi.org/10.3386/w23089

Altunbas, F. (2013). *Social media in policing: A study of Dallas-Fort Worth area city police departments*. University of North Texas.

Asano, E. (2017). How much time do people spend on social media? *Social Media Today*. www.socialmediatoday.com/marketing

Campbell, D., & Fiske, D. (1959). Convergent and discriminant validation by the multitrait-multimethod matrix. *Psychological Bulletin*, *56*(2), 81–105.

Cohen, L. (2010). *6 ways law enforcement uses social media to fight crime*. http://connectedcops.net/wp-content/uploads/2010/04/6-Ways-Law-Enforcement-Uses-Social-Media-to-Fight-Crime.pdf

Dai, M., He, W., Tian, X., Giraldi, A., & Gu, F. (2017). Working with communities on social media: Varieties in the use of Facebook and Twitter by local police. *Online Information Review*, *41*(6), 782–796. https://doi.org/10.1108/OIR-01-2016-0002

Denef, S., Bayerl, P. S., & Kaptein, N. A. (2013). Social media and the police: Tweeting practices of British police forces during the August 2011 riots. In P. Grinter, T. Rodden, P. Aoki, E. Cutrell, R. Jeffries, & G. Olson (Eds.), *Proceedings of the SIGCHI conference on human factors in computing systems* (pp. 3471–3480). Association for Computing Machinery.

Denef, S., Kaptein, N., Bayerl, S., & Ramirez, L. (2012). *Best practice in police social media adaptation*. http://hdl.handle.net/1765/40562

Denzin, N. (2009). *The research act: A theoretical introduction to sociological methods*. Routledge. https://doi.org/10.4324/9781315134543

Duncombe, C. (2011). *The Twitter revolution? Social media, representation and crisis in Iran and Libya*. Australian Political Science Association Conference (APSA 2011), Australian National University, School of Politics and International Relations, Canberra, Australia, 26–28 September 2011.

Esfandiari, G. (2010). The Twitter devolution. *Foreign Policy*. https://foreignpolicy.com/2010/06/08/the-twitter-devolution/

Gębarska, D., & Sobocińska, J. (2022, in press). *Niesłuszne skazania w Polsce. Badania ankietowe wśród polskich sędziów* [Master thesis defended at the University of Warsaw].

Hern, A. (2018). Cambridge Analytica: How did it turn clicks into votes? *The Guardian*. www.theguardian.com/news/2018/may/06/

Hu, X., & Lovrich, N. P. (2020). Electronic Community-Oriented Policing Theories, Contemporary Efforts, and Future Directions, Lexington Books.
Jasiński, W. (2015). *Polish criminal process after the reform*. Helsińska Fundacja Praw Człowieka. www.statewatch.org/media/documents/news/2015/jul/poland-criminal-process-after-reform.pdf
Jungblut, M., Kümpel, A. S., & Steer, R. (2022). Social media use of the police in crisis situations: A mixed-method study on communication practices of the German police. *New Media & Society*, *0*(0), 1–22. https://doi.org/10.1177/14614448221127899
Kemp, S. (2023). *Digital 2023 deep-dive: How much time do we spend on social media?* Dataportal. https://datareportal.com/reports/digital-2023-deep-dive-time-spent-on-social-media
Meijer, A., & Thaens, M. (2013). Social media strategies: Understanding the differences between North American police departments. *Government Information Quarterly*, *30*(4), 343–350. https://doi.org/10.1016/j.giq.2013.05.023
O'Keeffe, G. S., & Clarke-Pearson, K. (2011). The impact of social media on children, adolescents, and families. *Pediatrics, 127*(4), 800–804. https://doi.org/10.1542/peds.2011-0054
Olson, P. (2016). How Facebook helped Donald Trump become president. *Forbes*. www.forbes.com/sites/parmyolson/2016/11/09/how-facebook-helped-donald-trumpbecome-president/#2e1823c159c5
Rønn, K. V., Rasmussen, B., Roer, T. S., & Megan, C. (2021). On the perception and use of information from social media in investigative police work: Findings from a Scandinavian study. *Policing: A Journal of Policy and Practice*, *15*(2), 1262–1273. https://doi.org/10.1093/police/paaa028
Rosen, C. (2007). Virtual friendship and the new narcissism. *The New Atlantis, 17*, 15–31.
Schneider, C. J. (2016). *Policing and social media: Social control in an era of new media*. Lexington Books.
Statista. (2023a). *Number of internet and social media users worldwide as of October 2023*. www.statista.com/statistics/617136/digital-population-worldwide/
Statista. (2023b). *Number of monthly active Facebook users worldwide as of 3rd quarter 2023*. www.statista.com/statistics/264810/number-of-monthly-active-facebook-users-worldwide/
Stepanova, E. (2011). The role of information communication technologies in the "Arab spring". *Ponars Eurasia*, *159*, 1–6.
Stevens, L. (2010). Social media in policing: Nine steps for success. *The Police Chief*, *77*(2).
Wall, D. S., & Williams, M. L. (2013). Policing cybercrime: Networked and social media technologies and the challenges for policing. *Policing and Society*, *23*(4), 409–412. https://doi.org/10.1080/10439463.2013.780222
Walsh, J. P., & O'Connor, C. (2019). Social media and policing. A review of recent research. *Sociology Compass*, *13*(1). https://doi.org/10.1111/soc4.12648

Waszkiewicz, P. (Ed.). (2021). *Media społecznościowe w pracy organów ścigania*. Wydawnictwo INP PAN. https://doi.org/10.5281/zenodo.4624922

Waszkiewicz, P. (Ed.). (2022). *Media społecznościowe w postępowaniu karnym*. Wydawnictwo INP PAN. https://doi.org/10.5281/zenodo.6497415

Webb, E. J., Campbell, D. T., Schwartz, R. D., & Sechrest, L. (1966). *Unobtrusive measures: Nonreactive measures in the social sciences*. Rand McNally and Co.

Wolfsfeld, G., Segev, E., & Sheafer, T. (2013). Social media and the Arab spring: Politics comes first. *The International Journal of Press/Politics*, *18*(2), 115–137. https://doi.org/10.1177/1940161212471716

2 The online frontier

Social media use by law enforcement personnel in Poland

Stanisław Rabczuk

Introduction

The first account of social media use by law enforcement dates from October 2005, when campus police used Facebook photos and videos of students to track down offenders – in this case, fans of rival football teams in the United States who had started a near-riot after a game (Hodge, 2006, p. 95). A thorough examination of social media content led to the positive identification of over 50 lawbreakers (Hodge, 2006, p. 95). As new tools started to be used by law enforcement personnel, cases including social media gained more publicity. One example was the arrest of 14 Brower Boys juvenile gang members in 2012, made thanks to the observation of suspects' profiles on social media (Epstein, 2012). At that time such use of these platforms was a novelty, considering that only one-third of the world's population was present on social networking sites (Search Engine Watch, 2012). The same year, LexisNexis released the results of a survey in which 67% of law enforcement professionals claimed that information obtained through social media could help solve investigations more quickly (LexisNexis, 2012, p. 9). Sworn officers pointed out that social media serves, among other things, as a source for evidence collection and criminal identification and as a tool for crime prevention (LexisNexis, 2012, pp. 14–15).

At the time of writing (June 2023), almost 60% of people worldwide use social networks (DataReportal – Global Digital Insights, n.d.). Given the current popularity of social networking sites, their usage for crimefighting purposes is a natural choice for police departments all over the world. Social media may be used by officers in a variety of ways – sometimes manually, but also with the use of automated tools.

It is a fact that social media is present in courtrooms and police stations across the world. As highlighted in a summary report by the Congressional Research Service, there are two main purposes of social media use by law enforcement: communication and investigation (Congressional Research Service, 2022). When social media is used as a source of evidence, there are concerns regarding its admissibility in court (Angus-Anderson, 2015; Greene, 2019). In the United States, the case law of Maryland and Texas

DOI: 10.4324/9781032680194-2
This chapter has been made available under a CC-BY-NC 4.0 license.

courts led to the establishment of new criteria to be met by such evidence prior to its admission. Doubts arose in connection with the methods used for securing social media data and the supporting evidence necessary to establish a link between the data and the purported author (Angus-Anderson, 2015). The complexity of social media is also evident in its use for public communication. Many police departments use social media to communicate with the public. Hu et al. (2018) studied 14 profiles, the most popular at the time, run by American police departments; they concluded that the use of Facebook may help facilitate police–public relations and fight crime. Social media can also be a useful tool for police forces in crisis situations, from riots to natural disasters (Denef et al., 2013; Jungblut et al., 2022). M. A. Wood (2020) has researched the ways in which memes can be used to humanize police officers and create a sense of relatability between police and the public. He found that adequate use of such attractive posts, not necessarily strictly related to law enforcement, may foster page growth and help achieve greater reach. Hence, the potential uses of social media appear to be very broad, and applying it to both public policing and criminal investigation seems to be a natural choice for law enforcement; this chapter focuses on the latter purpose. It fills the gap in existing research by presenting the results of two studies that aimed at exploring the use of social media by Polish prosecutors and police officers as an investigative tool.

The next section provides a context for the research by referring to the existing literature on the topic. This is followed by a survey and discussion of the main findings of the study on the use of social media by prosecutors. These are compared with previous research conducted in 2019 with police officers (Bitner & Bayer, 2019; Czekalska & Krawczyk, 2021). Finally, the findings of the research are placed within the framework of social learning theory.

Not only for memes – police use of social media for crimefighting

A survey conducted among 500 law enforcement agencies in the United States in 2013 by the International Association of Chiefs of Police found that Facebook was the most commonly used social media platform for investigative purposes, with 86% of agencies reporting that they had used it (International Association of Chiefs of Police, 2013, p. 11). The authors found that social media had been most useful in identifying suspects, followed by locating witnesses and gathering evidence. Officers used a variety of techniques, with most of them reviewing suspects' social media profiles as well as their overall activity. They also created fake profiles to gather information undercover or to review victims' activity. The majority of responding agencies reported having a written policy on the use of social media.

The following year, a study by Rüdiger and Rogus (2014) aimed to understand how German police officers perceived the use of social media, both personally and professionally. Most respondents confirmed that they used social media in their private lives; Facebook was the most popular platform. They were more likely to report that the main purpose of their use of social media was intelligence gathering, with crime investigation lagging behind information acquisition from the public and in-service training. Although police staff strongly agreed that every police trainee or student ought to be taught how to use social media, only 28% of them had received any kind of online or offline training.

A more widespread study, based on a survey of 352 respondents from 22 European countries, was conducted by Bayerl et al. in 2012 (Bayerl et al., 2017). This showed that European police officers generally had positive attitudes toward social media, with almost all respondents having experience of using these platforms (93.5%). Nearly half (48.7%) reported using social media both privately and professionally, with overall use for official purposes at 54.8%. The level of acceptance of the use of social media depended on an individual's role within the police force. As observed, official use was significantly lower in Europe than in the United States (54.8% in Bayerl et al. compared to 86% in the 2013 International Association of Chiefs of Police (IACP) survey). However, due to the non-representativeness of the study, this conclusion cannot be drawn unequivocally. A more recent study, conducted by Peters et al. in 2019, found that out of 111 Nigerian police personnel, 67.7% claimed they had established an account for both private and professional use, plus 24.3% solely for personal use and 8.1% exclusively for professional use (Peters & Ojedokun, 2019). Despite the general rise in the number of social media users and the almost seven-year gap between the above studies, police forces in different countries vary in their levels of adoption; this may be caused by sociocultural factors. Such a backlog needs to be noted, as it also justifies detailed research on social media use in different regions of the world.

All these studies used online surveys as their primary source of data and targeted police officers as research participants. Egawhary (2019) took different approach and analyzed internal policy documents and official guidance obtained through FOI requests to 46 police forces in the UK. Her aim was to explore surveillance forces. The study outlined five surveillance affordances: general community surveillance, encouraging community self-surveillance, managerial, peer-to-peer, and investigative surveillance. Egawhary found that monitoring and surveillance of social media activity varied between forces, ranging from free tools to enterprise software. She highlighted the need for increased training, supervision, and counter-surveillance practices and concluded by pointing to a commonly overlooked concern: that corporate monitoring is limited to information security regarding hackers, rather than the platforms themselves. Egawhary's study provides insight into specific guidelines for online investigations, written by and for police professionals, and is, therefore, a valuable indirect source of information on police practice. Although the application of guidelines may be insufficient, as they rarely have grounds in police action, as stated by Egawhary (2019, p. 90), this does not necessarily impair the cognitive value of such data. One such guideline, published by the National Police Chiefs' Council in 2020, stresses that, for example, relevant considerations must be taken into account when conducting Internet investigations, including interacting with social media using overt and covert profiles (Lloyd, 2020). Interestingly, open profiles used by law enforcement personnel must clearly indicate their use by the police and may be shared between investigators, even when used for investigative purposes. However, in the UK, due to legal restrictions, the systematic monitoring of an individual's account, even if it is open to the public, is covered by the need for further authorization. The use of covert profiles is also limited to justified cases.

Legal and ethical concerns regarding access to open-source data via social networking sites have also been raised by police professionals trying to translate traditional rules for police actions in physical spaces into the digital world (Rønn et al., 2021). K. Rønn and colleagues conducted a study involving 12 group interviews with a total of 49 informants from Danish, Norwegian, and Swedish police services. They found that in almost all types of criminal investigations, participants perceived information from social media as valuable. Mainly, they associated social networking sites with Facebook, Instagram, or Twitter and used them to conduct background checks on persons of interest (POIs) in ongoing investigations. The authors identified the following main purposes for using social media: identifying connections and relationships between POIs, determining their whereabouts, identifying stolen property, and determining the identities of POIs by comparing photos and other data. Although useful, the use of social media information was reported to be fraught with technical pitfalls, leading to a general fear of making mistakes. Investigators found the legal framework for digital investigations to be vague, leading them to feel that they were working in a gray area. Informants expressed the view that this seemingly unregulated part of investigative work needed a major overhaul. While regulatory challenges remained, a lack of operational guidance and proper training was also highlighted. Participants pointed out personal security concerns: even the use of a covert profile could, due to the algorithms used by social networking sites, result in the presence of POIs in friend suggestions on their private accounts. Therefore, the risk of exposure still seems to be unaddressed, at least to some extent.

Scholars have also explored the general need to regulate access to cross-border digital evidence, particularly in the context of the European Commission's proposal for an e-Evidence Regulation, taking into account social networking sites (for critical analysis of the proposal's impact assessment, see Vazquez Maymir, 2020). The main reason for this was undoubtedly the number of requests by law enforcement agencies to service providers in the United States. As noted in the impact assessment, Facebook and Google alone accounted for over 70% of the total number of requests to the top five service providers (European Commission, n.d.). Investigators mainly used the direct cooperation method to compel service providers to provide data; the use of mechanisms established by Mutual Legal Assistance Treaties was significantly less popular. Despite Maymir's justified criticism, the facts highlighted by the European Commission confirm the need for a unified approach to the collection of digital evidence.

Studies provide a complex picture of the use of social media by law enforcement. Of all the challenges posed by social media to European police officers, two seem to be crucial: the vague legal frameworks for social media activities and privacy concerns. Meanwhile, the proportion of investigators making official use of social media is lower than in the United States, raising the question of why this is. A possible explanation was provided by Bayerl et al. (2017), who found in their cross-national study that investigators who used social media for both professional and personal purposes were significantly more positive in their attitudes toward it than non-users and private users only; frequent users were also significantly more positive than infrequent users.

Police use of social media in Poland – findings from the 2019 study

The findings section refers to a 2019 study,[1] which employed the method of structured interviews. Although its results have already been published (Bitner & Bayer, 2019; Czekalska & Krawczyk, 2021), they are not available to non-Polish speakers; they are therefore briefly discussed below, as they can provide an insight into the general view of social media use among law enforcement personnel in Poland. These findings will be employed here to foster discussion on the use of social media by prosecutors.

From October 2018 to February 2019, an exploratory study was conducted on the use of social media by officers from the Warsaw Police Department. A total of 67 participants were interviewed in person; they varied in age (mean = 37.5; median = 38), seniority, and position. The sample consisted mostly of officers with between 3 and 15 years of experience (3 to 10 – 38.81%; 11 to 15 – 37.32%); this is in line with statistics on the general numbers of police personnel in Poland. One-third of the participants worked in the investigation department of their local police (Czekalska & Krawczyk, 2021, p. 49). In general, 43 of them (64.18%) reported using social media at work. Although

1 The present author participated in designing the study and conducting the interviews with police officers. The other members of the research team were Katarzyna Bayer, Jan Bitner, Marta Czekalska, Hubert Dębniak, Karolina Fabrycka, Dominika Hoinca, Aleksandra Jędrzejak, Paulina Kargul, Kinga Krawczyk, Karolina Mazur, Michał Mazur, Karolina Skraba, Ignacy Strzałkowski, and Paweł Wasylkowski. The head of the team was Professor Paweł Waszkiewicz.

limited by the exploratory nature of the study and the non-representative sample, Bayer and Bitner found that personal use of social media did not appear to be related to service use. They also found no relationship between seniority and work-related use of social media. However, they did find evidence of an association between attending social media training and using it at work (Bitner & Bayer, 2019, p. 30).

Research questions and hypothesis

The extensive use and wide possibilities of the application of social media in police work naturally demand further exploration. However, the majority of studies on social media use by police have been conducted outside of Europe; there is a lack of up-to-date literature, both qualitative and quantitative, set in a European context. A number of studies have focused on police departments' use of social media for communicating with the public instead of its possible use in investigations. Moreover, the available studies have overlooked prosecutors as participants, thus missing a valuable source of information about the applicability of social media in criminal investigations.

We[2] found prosecutors to be relevant objects of study because of their specific position in the Polish criminal process. Due to their superior role over the police – they supervise their actions in the process of criminal investigation – they have the exclusive right to make crucial procedural decisions, such as indictment (Bulenda et al., 2006). Therefore, unlike in some countries, Polish prosecutors are actively involved in the investigation phase of criminal proceedings. They are thus aware of the challenges faced not only by themselves but also by those they supervise. Also, unlike police officers, they participate in criminal proceedings, present evidence in court, and argue the case against the defendant; this gives them a unique perspective on the suitability of social media evidence in the court phase of criminal proceedings.

As the 2019 study targeted officers from the Warsaw Police Department, we decided to design countrywide research including prosecutors as participants. To paint a wider picture of social media use by Polish law enforcement agencies, I will include the discussion findings of Bitner & Bayer (2019), as well as Czekalska and Krawczyk (2021). Two research questions were drawn up for the study sample of prosecutors:

RQ1: Which social networking sites are used by prosecutors in criminal investigations?

2 The author participated in designing the study and conducting the interviews with prosecutors. The other members of the research team were Magda Tomaszewska-Michalak and Błażej Stromczyński. The head of the team was Professor Paweł Waszkiewicz.

RQ2: Of those who refuse to use social media, why are they reluctant?

Several hypotheses specific to prosecutors were also formulated:

H1: The majority of prosecutors will use social media for investigative purposes.
H2: Those prosecutors who frequently use social media for private purposes will be more likely to use it for official purposes.
H3: Prosecutors who refrain from official use of social media will generally do so because of privacy concerns.

Method and limitations

When studying law enforcement, the relevant limitation is the reluctance of agencies to share their data, due to the concern that some of the information provided may negatively impact crimefighting efforts. Egawhary (2019) pointed out that at the time of writing her paper, only few of the requested reports regarding police practice were provided unredacted. Police agencies pointed to concerns that knowledge of how investigative work is carried out on social media platforms could lead to "catastrophic damage" (Egawhary, 2019). Therefore, in our study, we had to use appropriate safeguards to mitigate the risk of agencies refusing to cooperate. We designed our research to collect data on law enforcement personnel's use of social media only in the context of overt actions, with an emphasis on collection methods for digital evidence. The following section describes in detail the method employed in our study.

We decided to employ structured interviews. This type of interview is a popular research method used to collect data in a systematic and structured way. Our choice was based on the idea of ensuring the possibility of future hypothesis testing (Kvale & Brinkmann, 2009, p. 106). The method used involved asking participants a predetermined set of questions in a face-to-face setting. The goal was to obtain accurate information from participants in a standardized manner that would allow easy comparison and analysis of the data collected.

To ensure the reliability and validity of the data collected, we followed strict procedures in conducting the interviews. All four interviewers[3] were trained in the interview technique and provided with a standardized set of questions for the participants. We also conducted pilot interviews to test the interview questions and refine the process.

3 The author, Paweł Waszkiewicz, Magda Tomaszewska-Michalak, and Błażej Stromczyński.

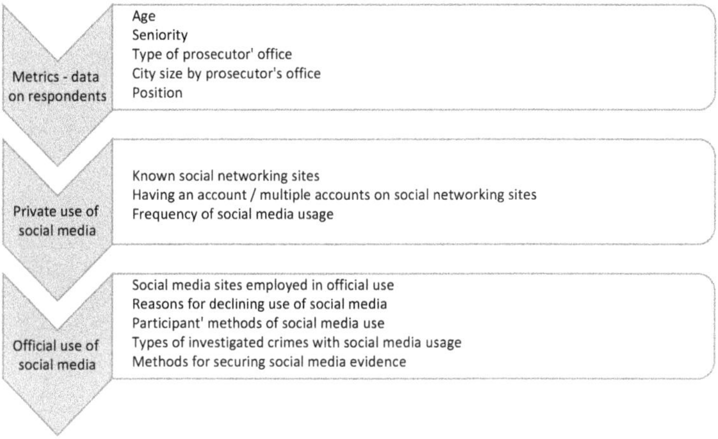

Figure 2.1 Overview of structured interview

The interview questions (see Figure 2.1), both closed and open-ended, were designed to explore various aspects of social media use in criminal investigations, including the types of social media platforms used, the purposes for which social media was used, and how such digital evidence was secured. The interviewers conducted the study one-on-one with each participant, with each interview lasting approximately 20 minutes. Respondents' answers were manually noted during the interview and stored using an online questionnaire.

Sample

In total, we interviewed participants from 22 different prosecutors' offices across the country (see Figure 2.2) between June 2021 and April 2022. First, we randomly selected prosecutors' offices for the study; we then randomly selected participants based on their availability. In 2020, there were 5,800 prosecutors in Poland (Council of Europe, 2022, p. 106). The study included a sample of 116 participants, with a margin of error of ±9% at the 95% confidence level (Qualtrics, 2023). The participants were diverse in terms of age, experience, and the type of unit in which they served (see Table 2.1).

Only ten respondents were appointed as assistant prosecutors, which is a temporary position for a maximum of three years before the final appointment as a prosecutor. Most of the participants were appointed as prosecutors of the district prosecutor's office (69), prosecutors of the county prosecutor's office (23), or prosecutors of the regional prosecutor's office (14).

Figure 2.2 A map showing the location of each prosecutor's office and the provinces covered by the study

Table 2.1 Sample description by age, type of office, and seniority

Age		*Type of office*		*Seniority*	
<30	2	District prosecutors' office	77	<3	12
31–40	33	Circuit prosecutors' office	29	3–10	21
41–50	57	Regional prosecutors' office	10	11–15	33
>50	24	*Total*	*116*	16–20	14
Total	*116*			21–30	25
				>30	11
				Total	*116*

Results

Prosecutors' use of social media for investigation

A majority (83.62%) of prosecutors were committed to using social networks in their investigative work (see Table 2.2.); H1 was therefore confirmed. Out of 116 participants, 97 reported using social networking sites, with Facebook clearly in the lead (see Table 2.3.). The number of prosecutors using social media did not correlate with training, as only 15 of them (12.93%) admitted having attended some kind of workshop on new technologies, not necessarily exclusively on social media. Although only two of those who had attended training did not use social media for professional purposes, the difference between the trained and untrained samples was not statistically significant (two-tailed p-value greater than 0.75).

The most popular social networking site for use by prosecutors in investigations was Facebook, followed by Instagram and Twitter. Other sites mentioned were YouTube, Snapchat, LinkedIn, TikTok, Telegram, Nk.pl, Fotka.pl, and 6obcy.org (see Table 2.3.).

Active social media users and work-related use

Bayerl et al. (2017) found that investigators who were frequent users of social media for private purposes were significantly more positive about using social networking sites at work. In H2, it was expected that prosecutors who were active users of social media would be more likely to opt-in to official use. Active users were classified as those who reviewed social media notifications promptly; participants who reported private social media use were asked to rate how quickly they became familiar with new notifications. Those who checked their accounts at least a few times a day were considered active users. Two individuals declined to answer this question and were therefore dropped from the sample ($n = 75$).

Of those who were considered active users, only 83% reported using social media at work, compared to nearly 97% of less-active users (with a

Table 2.2 Current social media use by prosecutors

Type of use	*Number of prosecutors*	*% Share*		
Private use only	8	6.90%	**Private use 66.38%**	
Official and private use	69	59.48%		**Official use 83.62%**
Work-related use only	28	24.14%		
No use at all	11	9.48%		

Table 2.3 Social networking sites reported by prosecutors as used in investigations

Social networking site	*Number of responses*	*% share*
Facebook	87	*67,97%*
Instagram	15	*11,72%*
Twitter	5	*3,9%*
Other	21	*16,41%*

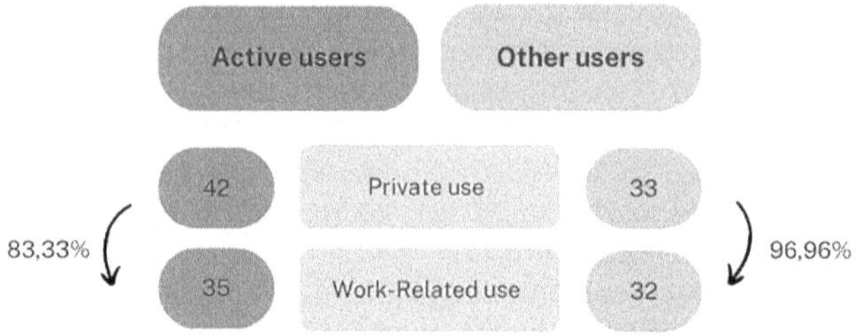

Figure 2.3 Active social networking site users and their use of these sites for criminal investigations

two-tailed *p*-value of 0.419; see Figure 2.3.). The results are interpreted as inconclusive, as there is insufficient evidence to support Hypothesis 2 (For the reasons why the *p*-value does not serve as a marker for accepting hypotheses, see Greenland et al., 2016, p. 341).

"I don't know how to use the Internet"

Of the 19 prosecutors who did not use social media as part of their investigative work, 18 provided an explanation for why they did not do so. Through the method of thematic analysis, it was possible to gain insight into the experiences and perspectives of the research participants by systematically identifying and organizing patterns of meaning within their responses (Clarke & Braun, 2017). We[4] first familiarized ourselves with the data, coded it, and then grouped the codes into overarching themes (Maguire & Delahunt, 2017). To avoid possible distortion of the data, the coding was done separately by two native Polish speakers, who later agreed on the final results. After the process was completed, the themes, subthemes, and examples were translated into English. All italicized quotes in this section are verbatim interviewee responses. In total, three major themes were identified, with six accompanying subthemes. Because some responses encompassed more than one theme, the total number of subthemes was greater than the number of participants.

The most popular subthemes identified in participants' responses were lack of Internet access, prohibitions on using social networking sites from their work PCs, lack of skills, and anticipated lack of applicability of social media in the type of investigation being conducted. A general lack of knowledge about the use of social media and Internet technologies was expressed by five prosecutors; the same number conveyed a belief in the lack of applicability of social

4 The author and Marta Banach.

Table 2.4 Themes and subthemes identified from prosecutors' answers to a question regarding their reasons for declining to use social media for crimefighting purposes

Themes	*Subthemes*	*Description of subthemes*	*Example*
Organizational capabilities	No Internet access ($n = 5$)	Lack of internet access at prosecutors' desks	*We don't have Internet access here, in the prosecutor's office.*
	No official account ($n = 1$)	Lack of official accounts available for prosecutors to conduct searches	*We do not have an account that could be used for official use.*
Personal skills and believes	Lack of skills ($n = 5$)	General lack of knowledge about the use of social media and internet technologies	*I don't know anything about the Internet. I don't know how to use it.*
	Personal security concerns ($n = 2$)	Concerns about revealing the identity of prosecutors	*For security reasons. I don't have an account as then I would be easy to track down.*
Lack of applicability in the investigation	Type of investigated case ($n = 5$)	Lack of applicability of social media to certain types of investigations conducted by prosecutors	*There is no need to use it in cases which I am handling (white-collar crimes).*
	Competence of other forces ($n = 4$)	Perception that other agencies, such as the police, should be responsible for the collection of evidence through the use of social media methods	*I generally outline the task in the guidelines for the police, and they choose how they will implement it. They are the ones who use it, and I don't get involved.*

networking sites to the specific types of cases they handled. Only two respondents indicated that they did not use social media because of security concerns; therefore, no evidence was found to support H3. There were, however, some unexpected reasons why prosecutors did not use social media, as well as other open sources in general. Five participants explained that their work computers were not connected to the Internet for security reasons. In some prosecutors' offices, there is usually a single or limited number of computers with such access in the shared office, but basic websites are blocked even on those:

> *I don't have such ability. I have limited Internet access; I can only access selected sites. I don't have access to social media sites, nor even to the National Court Register.*
>
> (Interviewee 2)

This was an alarmingly widespread phenomenon: during the interviews, 41 participants stated that there were no devices suitable for the use of social media in their offices, and another 23 reported that there were only shared computers or other devices with blocked access to social media sites. There were, therefore, 64 prosecutors (55.17%) who did not have the ability to browse the Internet freely.

Discussion

As stated, 83.62% of prosecutors declared work-related use of social media. This was greater than the declared use of social media by officers from the Warsaw Police Department (64.18%) (Bitner & Bayer, 2019, pp. 20–21) and the results of the 2012 study by Bayerl et al. (2017) (54.8%). It may be assumed that during the decade that passed between the cited research and our research, the general number of social media users increased significantly, which led to greater recognition of social networking sites among prosecutors and police officers. Moreover, there has been an increase in the share of older people among Facebook users (in the United States, the share of users aged 55–64 rose from 6% in 2012 to 11.1% by 2023; there is a lack of comparable data for Polish users (see pingdom.com, n.d.; Statista, n.d.). Also, the last few years have been crucial for law enforcement agencies in Poland, with a significant rise in the number of requests for data from major social media providers. Reports from Facebook support our assumption that between the 2019 study of Polish police officers and the 2021/2 study of prosecutors, more law enforcement agencies started to recognize social media as a tool supporting criminal investigations, which may explain why a higher proportion of prosecutors reported using social media. Between 2018 and 2022, the number of data release requests tripled, from around 2,000 per year to 6,000 (Government Requests for User Data | Transparency Center, n.d.).

Our opinion that using social media privately seems unrelated to service use is consistent with the observations of Bayer and Bitner (2019, p. 21). It, therefore, appears that for Polish law enforcement personnel, this variable does not play a crucial role. Prosecutors do not necessarily need to establish an account on a social networking site in order to utilize it in a criminal investigation. They are free to perform online searches without one and secure evidence from publicly accessible sources. They also tend to request data from service providers;

this is recognized by them as a means of using social media to obtain evidence through subpoenas.

However, contrary to Bayer and Bitner (2019, p. 30), who found that training of police personnel fostered the use of social media at stations, there was insufficient evidence for such a conclusion in the case of prosecutors. One possible explanation is that participants simply learned about the potential uses of social media from their peers (prosecutors and police officers) on the road. However, this does not excuse the government from its obligation to provide appropriate training. The reported use of social media does not distinguish the degree to which these tools are used by prosecutors, and such levels may vary depending on training.

Possibly the most surprising finding, not yet identified in foreign studies, may be the lack of basic organizational capacities in Polish prosecutors' offices. Bayer and Bitner (2019, p. 32) found similar evidence: in their interviews, a significant number of police officers emphasized that police-owned devices were rarely available for Internet browsing, and those that were had to be shared among investigators (Bitner & Bayer, 2019, p. 32). Therefore, it seems that this organizational backlog is typical for Polish law enforcement agencies. An often-repeated excuse is that some restrictions on Internet access need to be enforced due to security concerns. However, nowadays, with the wide applicability of OSINT use in investigations, such organizational challenges can be solved by simply providing prosecutors with a second device connected to the Internet and not having access to internal data. This is especially important since one of the prosecutors who did not use social media due to lack of Internet access was one of the few who said he had received training in the use of Internet technologies.

Prosecutors' reasons for not using social media might relate to a lack of knowledge about its potential applicability in criminal cases. Also, the idea that the police are better placed to use social media seems to be caused by a lack of appropriate perspective. The use of social media to carry out specific covert operations against suspects falls within the traditional competencies of the police; however, its overt use, such as for searching and securing evidence, is an activity that can also be carried out by prosecutors to the benefit of the investigation.

Social learning (cognitive) theory, which considers how environmental and cognitive factors interact to influence human learning and behavior, may aid in further understanding the results of the study. The theory outlines four factors that foster individuals' engagement in a particular behavior (Vahedi, 2020, p. 403): first, performance outcomes – people are more likely to engage in a behavior if they have previous positive experience with the task. Other sources of self-efficacy are modeling (seeing other individuals succeed at a given task), social persuasion (positive or negative reinforcement received from others), and emotional arousal (experienced physiological sensations). In the example of law enforcement personnel, their own experience, as well as observed

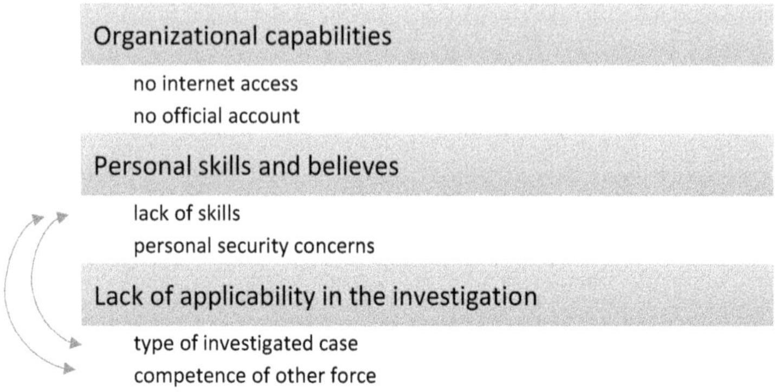

Figure 2.4 A diagram showing the possible relationships between the identified subthemes

experience, especially in their close peer group – for example, other prosecutors from their office – may influence their decisions to use social media in investigations.

Those who have previously failed to use social media effectively may be more reluctant to do so in the future. One such example is receiving a refusal to share data from a social media provider; such a circumstance is a negative experience, which represents potentially reduced commitment to a process when investigating different crimes. Counteractive measures may include dissemination of official information about the number of approved requests by particular providers in order to provide context and broad perspective for the investigator. Self-efficacy may also be related to confidence in one's own digital investigative skills. Law enforcement personnel's self-perceived proficiency in utilizing social media for investigations may influence their willingness to incorporate these techniques into their investigative toolkit. A majority (83.62%) of prosecutors were committed to using social networks in their investigative work (see Figure 2.4.).

Social learning theory puts emphasis on observing other individuals, especially those to whom one can relate; this shows the importance of law enforcement personnel's evaluations of their colleagues. Prosecutors may believe that social media is not applicable to certain types of investigations because they have not seen others using it in similar cases. Similarly, police officers in Poland expressed their skepticism toward social media by deprecating their own skills and manifesting their attachment to old-school methods of policing (Czekalska & Krawczyk, 2021, p. 56). This, however, may be addressed by providing them with case studies and examples of successful application of social media in criminal investigations. Social media use by police officers and prosecutors could also be fostered by positive reinforcement from supervisors, who should reward the active use of new technologies in fighting crime. Thus, there needs to be a change from top to bottom, as prosecutors supervise the actions of police officers; due to power-related bonds, they could potentially have a stronger influence on police personnel.

Conclusions

While social media can be a valuable tool for law enforcement in criminal investigations, it is important to use it responsibly and ethically. Proper training, policies, and guidelines are needed to ensure that it is used in a manner that respects the rights of individuals and the law. It is important for law enforcement agencies to be aware of potential concerns and to have policies and guidelines in place to address them.

This study highlights the importance of social media in investigative work and the need for adequate training and resources to enable prosecutors to use these platforms effectively. It has been found that Polish prosecutors include social media in their criminal investigations: 83% of participants reported doing so. However, the pattern differed from the study of Polish police officers. Contrary to the hypothesis, there was insufficient evidence found to support the notion that active private social media users are more likely to use it for official purposes. Also, it was found that training in new technologies did not significantly influence prosecutors' use of social media. Nonetheless, such training is necessary for prosecutors, given the varying degrees to which these tools are used in their work.

Thematic analysis of the reasons why some prosecutors did not use social media revealed several themes and provided more insights into such refusal. The most common reasons cited by prosecutors were a lack of Internet access or skills, and a belief that social media was not applicable to their investigations. Security concerns were mentioned by only a small number of respondents. Unexpectedly, some prosecutors reported that their work computers did not have Internet access or had limited Internet capabilities, which can be a significant obstacle to their investigative work. As the same obstacles were reported by the study group of police officers, the recommendation concerning organizational improvements in public prosecutors' offices may also be implemented at police stations.

By employing social learning theory, decision-makers may further understand the rationales behind prosecutors' and police officers' attitudes toward social media. The theory underscores four key determinants of behavior: performance outcomes, modeling, social persuasion, and emotional arousal. The potential impact of the first three on the decision-making processes of individuals has been highlighted above. A number of potential countermeasures can serve to address these challenges. By understanding the patterns of social media use among law enforcement personnel, authorities should aim to promote a more robust adoption of social media in investigative practices, especially since, in modern crimefighting, using social media seems to be part of the "101" chapter in the investigator's manual.

References

Angus-Anderson, W. (2015). Authenticity and admissibility of social media website printouts. *Duke Law & Technology Review*, *14*(1), 33–47.

Bayerl, S. P., Jacobs, G., & Horton, K. (2017). Ignoring, tolerating or embracing? Social media use in European police forces. *European Law Enforcement Research Bulletin, 2*(2), 295–308.

Bitner, J., & Bayer, K. (2019). Wykorzystanie mediów społecznościowych przez funkcjonariuszy polskiej Policji. Próba wstępnego opisu zjawiska na podstawie wyników badań kwestionariuszowych. In E. Gruza, T. Tomaszewski, & M. Goc (Eds.), *Problemy Współczesnej Kryminalistyki* (p. XXIII). Polish Forensic Association & Department of Criminalistics at the University of Warsaw.

Bulenda, T., Gruszczynska, B., Kremplewski, A., & Sobota, P. (2006). The prosecution service function within the polish criminal justice system. In J.-M. Jehle & M. Wade (Eds.), *Coping with overloaded criminal justice systems: The rise of prosecutorial power across Europe* (pp. 257–284). Springer. Retrieved May 7, 2023, from https://doi.org/10.1007/978-3-540-33963-2_8

Clarke, V., & Braun, V. (2017). Thematic analysis. *The Journal of Positive Psychology, 12*(3), 297–298. Routledge.

Congressional Research Service. (2022). *Law enforcement and technology: Using social media*. Retrieved March 5, 2023, from https://sgp.fas.org/crs/misc/R47008.pdf

Council of Europe. (2022). *European judicial systems CEPEJ evaluation report – 2022 evaluation cycle (2020 data)*. Council of Europe. Retrieved May 7, 2023, from https://rm.coe.int/cepej-fiche-pays-2020-22-e-web/1680a86276

Czekalska, M., & Krawczyk, K. (2021). Media społecznościowe jako narzędzie pracy polskiej Policji. Wyniki badań kwestionariuszowych. In *Media Społecznościowe w Pracy Organów Ścigania*. INP PAN.

DataReportal – Global Digital Insights. (n.d.). *Global social media statistics*. Retrieved February 25, 2023, from https://datareportal.com/social-media-users

Denef, S., Bayerl, P. S., & Kaptein, N. A. (2013). *Social media and the police: Tweeting practices of British police forces during the August 2011 riots*. Proceedings of the SIGCHI Conference on Human Factors in Computing Systems, Association for Computing Machinery, CHI'13, New York, NY, USA, 27 April 2013, pp. 3471–3480. Retrieved March 5, 2023, from https://doi.org/10.1145/2470654.2466477

Egawhary, E. M. (2019). The surveillance dimensions of the use of social media by UK police forces. *Surveillance & Society*, *17*(1–2), 89–104.

Epstein, E. A. (2012). *Rapping Brooklyn burglars caught after police friended them on Facebook . . . and they posted about their crimes*. Retrieved September 28, 2023, from www.dailymail.co.uk/news/article-2152484/Rapping-Brooklyn-burglars-caught-police-friended-Facebook-posted-crimes.html

European Commission. (n.d.). *Commission staff working document – impact assessment accompanying the document proposal for a regulation of the European parliament and of the council on European production and preservation orders for electronic evidence in criminal matters and proposal for a directive of the European parliament and of the council laying down harmonised rules on the appointment of legal representatives for the purpose of gathering evidence in criminal proceedings (SWD/2018/118 final)*. European Commission. Retrieved February 13, 2021, from https://eur-lex.europa.eu/legal-content/EN/TXT/?uri=SWD%3A2018%3A118%3AFIN

Government Requests for User Data | Transparency Center. (n.d.). Retrieved September 21, 2023, from https://transparency.fb.com/reports/government-data-requests/

Greene, L. (2019). Mining metadata: The gold standard for authenticating social media evidence in Illinois. *DePaul Law Review*, *68*(1).

Greenland, S., Senn, S. J., Rothman, K. J., Carlin, J. B., Poole, C., Goodman, S. N., & Altman, D. G. (2016). Statistical tests, P values, confidence intervals, and power: A guide to misinterpretations. *European Journal of Epidemiology*, *31*, 337–350.

Hodge, M. J. (2006). The fourth amendment and privacy issues on the new internet: Facebook.com and Myspace.com. *Southern Illinois University Law Journal*, 31, 95.

Hu, X., Rodgers, K., & Lovrich, N. P. (2018). "We are more than crime fighters": Social media images of police departments. *Police Quarterly*, *21*(4), 544–572.

International Association of Chiefs of Police. (2013). *IACP Social Media Survey Results* (p. 18). https://www.westdefense.com/wp-content/uploads/sites/1100252/2017/05/2013SurveyResults.pdf

Jungblut, M., Kümpel, A. S., & Steer, R. (2022). Social media use of the police in crisis situations: A mixed-method study on communication practices of the German police. In *New Media & Society*. SAGE. https://doi.org/10.14614448221127899

Kvale, S., & Brinkmann, S. (2009). *Interviews: Learning the craft of qualitative research interviewing*. SAGE.

LexisNexis. (2012). *Survey of law enforcement personnel and their use of social media in investigations*. https://risk.lexisnexis.com/insights-resources/infographic/2012-law-enforcement-use-of-social-media-report

Lloyd, P. (2020). *Internet intelligence & investigations strategy*. National Police Chiefs' Council. Retrieved May 5, 2023, from https://library.college.police.uk/docs/NPCC/Internet-Intelligence-and-Investigation-v1.5.pdf

Maguire, M., & Delahunt, B. (2017). Doing a thematic analysis: A practical, step-by-step guide for learning and teaching scholars. *All Ireland Journal of Higher Education, 9*(3), 3.

Peters, S. E., & Ojedokun, U. A. (2019). Social media utilization for policing and crime prevention in Lagos, Nigeria. *Journal of Social, Behavioral, and Health Sciences*, *13*(1).

pingdom.com. (n.d.). *Report: Social network demographics in 2012 – Pingdom*. Retrieved May 7, 2023, from www.pingdom.com/blog/report-social-network-demographics-in-2012/

Qualtrics. (2023). *Margin of error guide & calculator*. Retrieved October 11, 2023, from www.qualtrics.com/experience-management/research/margin-of-error/

Rønn, K. V., Rasmussen, B. K., Skou Roer, T., & Meng, C. (2021). On the perception and use of information from social media in investigative police work: Findings from a Scandinavian study. *Policing: A Journal of Policy and Practice*, *15*(2), 1262–1273.

Rüdiger, T.-G., & Rogus, M. (2014). *Survey on the use of social media by the German police*. University of Applied Sciences of the Police of Brandenburg.

Search Engine Watch. (2012). *Worldwide social media usage trends in 2012*. Retrieved February 25, 2023, from www.searchenginewatch.com/2012/12/26/worldwide-social-media-usage-trends-in-2012/

Statista. (n.d.). *U.S. Facebook demographics age 2023*. Retrieved May 7, 2023, from www.statista.com/statistics/187549/facebook-distribution-of-users-age-group-usa/

Vahedi, Z. (2020). Social learning theory/social cognitive theory. In *The Wiley encyclopedia of personality and individual differences* (pp. 401–405). John Wiley & Sons, Ltd. Retrieved October 11, 2023, from https://onlinelibrary.wiley.com/doi/abs/10.1002/9781119547143.ch67

Vazquez Maymir, S. (2020). Anchoring the need to revise cross-border access to e-evidence. *Internet Policy Review*. Epub ahead of print 2020. https://doi.org/10.14763/2020.3.1495

Wood, M. A. (2020). Policing's "meme strategy": Understanding the rise of police social media engagement work. *Current Issues in Criminal Justice*, *32*(1), 40–58. Routledge.

3 Paw patrol? How Polish police are using animal images and funny content on social media

Magdalena Tomaszewska-Michalak

Introduction

According to Statista, there were 5.03 billion Internet users worldwide in 2022. Among them, 4.7 billion were social media users (Statista, 2022c). Statista also predicts that the number of social media users will increase, reaching 5.85 billion in 2027 (Statista, 2022b). Other data show that a fair proportion (the percentage depends on the country) of social media users treat it as a source of information (Statista, 2022a). An interesting and vivid profile on social media may, therefore, be crucial for getting people's attention and boosting one's number of fan-page followers. While commercial brands' motivations for using social media are easy to recognize, it becomes more complicated when platforms such as Twitter or Facebook are used by public institutions. This chapter focuses on one such institution: the police. There are some guidelines in the literature on maintaining social media profiles by the police (e.g., IACP, 2019); there is, however, no single agreed strategy on this issue.

For the period explored in this research, Facebook seemed to be the leading social media platform used by police departments. Researchers claim that in the US, 96% of police departments maintain a profile on social media. Among them, 94% use Facebook (Hu et al., 2018). This is also true in countries with other legal cultures. Research in Poland has confirmed that if a particular Polish police department uses only one social media platform, that platform will be Facebook (Waszkiewicz et al., 2021).

State of the art

The literature points out several reasons why the police are using social media (e.g., Bayerl et al., 2017). In the last few years, the potential of social media has been recognized by the police themselves. This is expressed, for example, in a document issued by the International Association of Chiefs of Police (IACP), which lists several possible circumstances where police may use social media (IACP, 2019). First, it may be an investigative tool, especially when there is a need to gather information about a missing or wanted person. Second, it may

DOI: 10.4324/9781032680194-3
This chapter has been made available under a CC-BY-NC 4.0 license.

be used to get closer to the public by posting crime prevention tips, sharing data about crime statistics, or building trust based on mutual exchange of information. Third, social media may be a way to disseminate local news important for the community (e.g., weather conditions on roads, accidents). Police may also use social media as a recruitment tool or a credible source of information for media (e.g., by counteracting misinformation) (IACP, 2019).

Whatever reason a police department may have for using social media, the first step is to win followers who will interact with the uploaded content. More and more studies are trying to find the pattern for what makes a police social media profile popular with its audience. In the case of Facebook, attention is focused on both the content and form of uploaded posts. It is possible to identify several post types on Facebook: written content, links, photographs, and videos. Marketing research shows that uploaded videos are more engaging than other forms of content (Peters, 2019).

Scholars also focus on the content of Facebook posts. There are various ideas on how to categorize police Facebook posts based on content; although the main categories remain similar, there is no agreement on how many of them should be identified. For instance, Lieberman et al. (2013) propose a division into 12 main categories, whereas Hu et al. (2018) identify only 5. Some categories also contain subcategories. Despite these differences, the idea of classifying posts based on content allows the researcher to analyze audience engagement with uploaded posts provided by law enforcement agencies. It may also be helpful for finding the most suitable strategy to get social media followers.

One marketing strategy focuses on obtaining Facebook followers by placing memes and animal content posts on the fan page. Wood (2020a) analyzed this strategy via the example of the Facebook profile of the New South Wales Police Force (NSWP) in Australia. NSWP relied on marketing knowledge about Facebook's News Feed Algorithm; Facebook claims that this algorithm decides what to display on users' profiles based on a few factors. The most important of these is the identity of the uploader of the post (friends or institutions/companies followed by the user) and the possibility that a person will interact with a post (share it, click on a link, give it a "like") (How Facebook Distributes Content, 2022). Based on this, NSWP assumed that animal and funny content might be a good way to encourage an audience to follow the police fan page on Facebook (Wood, 2020a). Wood called this approach "meme strategy." Every post was an element of "meme strategy" if it was humorous, if an Internet meme was a part of it, or if it featured an animal image (Wood, 2020a). This strategy worked well: in 2017 the number of NSWP Facebook followers reached 1 million (Wood, 2020a), and in 2022, 1.4 million (NSW Police Force, 2022). Although NSWP achieved its goal, the idea of police forces using social media with the main aim of gathering followers has been criticized by some authors. First, there are some general concerns over the use of social media by law enforcement agencies. According to Livingstone (2022), the risks are improper use of social media, the necessity of dealing with social media crises after uploading posts, and privacy issues. Choosing an improper strategy for maintaining their social media profiles may also cause law enforcement agencies to lose credibility (Bullock, 2018). To gain the audience's attention, a social media profile should be interesting. Some authors, however, point out that for law enforcement agencies, their marketing strategy should be in accordance with their main goals as police forces (Liam, 2022); that is, preventing and investigating crimes and strengthening community policing. Finding the right balance between being a formal institution and communicating informally on social media is h not always easy. Even police officers have different opinions on the proper use of social media. A study of Scottish police showed that some officers consider that employing formal language on social media is necessary to maintain the authority of a public institution. Others claim that police legitimacy is built when the institution shows its human side (Liam, 2022). It seems there is no agreement on the necessary elements of building police legitimacy on social media. There are, however, instructions that aim to help law enforcement agencies maintain their social media profiles properly. IACP (2019) highlights the necessity of neutral content that avoids statements of guilt or innocence and does not comment on pending cases; it also mentions the need to not disclose confidential information on social media, and makes a vague reference to appropriate conduct. It does not refer, however, to the level of formality that the fan page should adopt. Oglesby-Neal and Warnberg (2019) encourage law enforcement agencies to create social media policy documents. These should specify, among other things, the tone of uploaded content (formal/informal) and the possibility of the use of humor.

Decisions on how to use humor and informal language are usually left to the police department that is responsible for establishing and maintaining a social media profile. Therefore, the strategies differ and are not always accepted by all police units, even within the same country. "Meme strategy" seems to have been very effective in gathering and keeping followers for one law enforcement agency (Wood, 2020a). Thus, the aim of this chapter is to analyze if this model is also used by Polish police and if it is an effective way to gather followers.

Study

This study aims to explore a strategy – "funny and cute content" – that may be used by Poland's law enforcement agencies to gather followers on Facebook. The idea is based on Wood's "meme strategy" (Wood, 2020a). However, there is no universal catalog that can be used to classify Facebook post content for every police department all over the world. The main categories are usually similar, but they have to be adapted to the conditions prevailing in a given country. Therefore, it is crucial to understand which posts are included in the "funny and cute content" strategy. Taking into account police literature, the Polish legal culture, and sociocultural background, we decided to distinguish 16 main content categories and 19 subcategories; these are shown in Table 3.1.

Three of these categories and subcategories were part of this research. The first two were linked with animal images: K9 and Service Horse. The first category, K9, was defined by coding researchers as *any posts containing information about a police dog or its image. If any other content, including funny content, contains a police dog, then the post should be classified under this category*.

The second category, Service Horse, was coded as *any posts containing information about a service horse or its image. If any other content, including funny content, contains a service horse, then the post should be classified under this category*.

The third category included in this analysis was Funny Content Linked with Police Work. The description of this category was *any content intended*

Table 3.1 Categories and subcategories of post content

Categories	*Subcategories*
Crime statistics	
Case	Case closed
	Cold case
	Potential case
DUI	
Tips	Crime prevention tips
	Prevention of victimization
Newsletter	Event
	Sport
	Personal achievements
	Charity
	Online events
Memorial	
Ask for help	
Police-linked content	Funny content
	Other content
Police non-linked content	Thanks to the police
	Other content
Law enforcement officer	Introduction
	Injured/sick/killed
	Misbehavior
Civilian employees	
K9	
Service Horse	
Recruitment	Direct
	Indirect
Other social media	
Other posts	

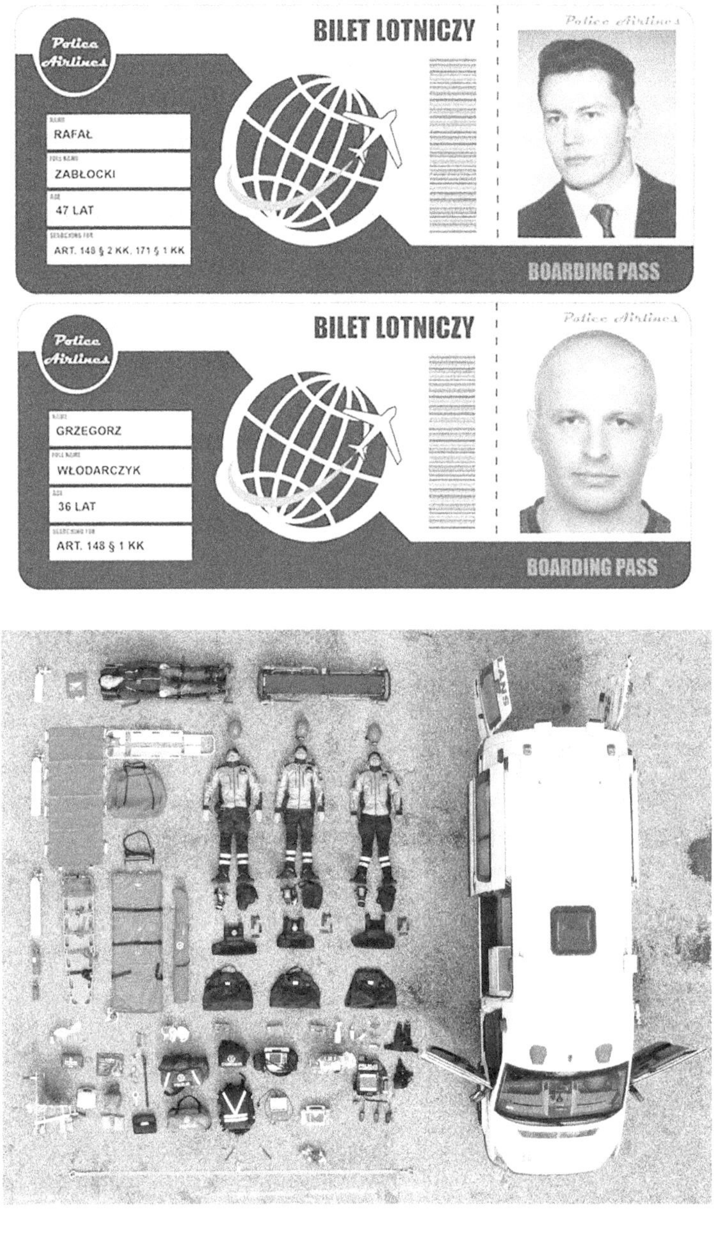

Image 3.1 Posts representing the Funny Content category: (a) Police Airlines free plane ticket for a wanted person (by Podkarpacka Policja). (b) Police Tetris challenge (by Policja Świętokrzyska)

Image 3.2 Posts representing the K9 category: (a) Police from Prudnik visit a kindergarten with dog Foksi (by Opolska Policja). (b) New dog in a police department (by Śląska Policja)

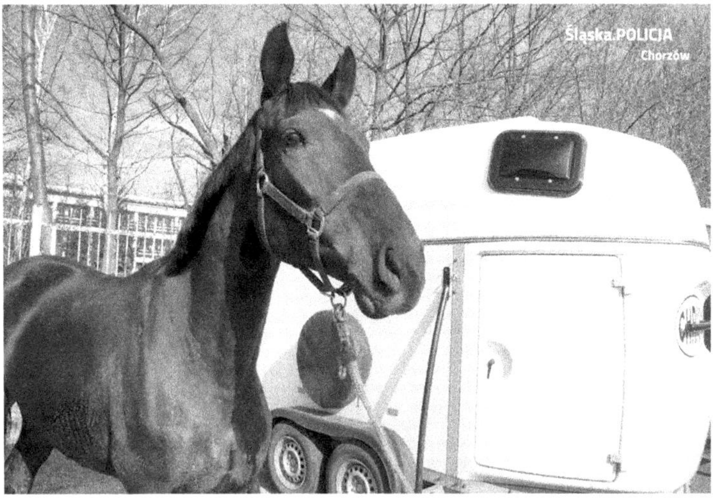

Image 3.3 Posts representing the Service Horse category: (a) New horse in a police department (by Policja Śląska). (b) The international police horse riding competition (by Policja Śląska)

to amuse the user, including memes and funny videos that contain a police element. Funny content not having a police element in it is not a part of this category. All three categories include the "funny and cute content" strategy. Images 3.1–3.3 are visual examples of posts from the categories K9, Service Horse, and Funny Content.

Hypothesis

The first research question focuses on the general use of posts categorized as "funny and cute content" by law enforcement agencies in Poland. The author intends to verify the hypothesis:

H1: *Polish police will use "funny and cute content" to increase the popularity of their Facebook profiles.*

As mentioned earlier, the literature only gives tips about how police should use social media. As there are no standardized instructions, law enforcement agencies all over the world introduce their own ad hoc ideas on how to gain audiences for their Facebook fan pages. One successful strategy has turned out to be uploading posts with animals (cute content) and funny content (Wood, 2020a). The author intends to verify if the Polish police are also using this strategy to expand their audience. The hypothesis will be verified in two ways: first, the number of "funny and cute content" posts in comparison to all other posts gathered during the research period. Second, for a broader context, the analysis will include two Polish provincial police departments: the one with the highest number of likes (Wielkopolska Policja) and the one with the lowest number of likes (Zachodniopomorska Policja).

H2: *Posts belonging to the "funny and cute content" categories will have more engagement activities than other posts.*

The idea behind the "funny and cute content" strategy is to get users more involved and, in consequence, to encourage more people to follow a police department's fan page. For the period of research, being engaged in Facebook content meant that a user was sharing a post, liking it, or clicking on a link. The hypothesis will be verified in two ways. First, I will analyze the general engagement with posts from categories included in "funny and cute content." Second, I will verify if the hypothesis is true for each category (K9, Service Horse, Funny Content) separately. For a broader context, the analysis will include two Polish provincial police departments: the one with the highest number of likes (Wielkopolska Policja) and the one with the lowest number of likes (Zachodniopomorska Policja).

Method/Data collection

The Polish police has a centralized structure. At the top there is a General Headquarters; then, there are 17 provincial police departments. In most cases, the areas of operation of provincial police departments coincide with those of voivodships. At the time of data collection, the provincial police departments were overseeing 336 district departments. After analyzing the available data, it turned out that by 2019, all provincial departments had Facebook accounts, whereas only 24% of district departments had established a profile on social media. The data from provincial police departments were then chosen for further analysis. Quite often, web crawlers are used to gather data; however, this method was not the best way to achieve the intended goal. Scraping data from Facebook gives only basic information about the posts uploaded by the entity in charge of a profile; it omits the important data, which on Facebook are called "Insights." Facebook Insights include not only posts but also all the statistics available to the profile administrator, such as Lifetime Post Total Reach, Lifetime Engaged Users, Lifetime Total Likes, Daily New Likes and Daily Unlikes, Daily Viral Reach, Total Video Views, Total Video Complete Views, Lifetime Video View Time, and Lifetime Negative Feedback. Three of these categories need to be explained as they will be used in the analysis. Lifetime Post Total Reach is the number of users who saw the page's post on their screens. Lifetime Engaged Users is the number of users who have engaged with a post. This engagement may take various forms, such as liking or sharing a post, leaving a comment, or clicking on an element of a post. Lifetime Negative Feedback is the number of people who react negatively to a post, which may mean clicking the X button, Hide Post, Hide All Posts, or Report as Spam. To obtain the necessary Facebook Insights, the research team decided to use the provisions of the Access to Information Act (ATI), issued on September 6, 2001, Article 2, which gives every citizen access to public information. Public information should be provided by all public authorities and other entities performing public tasks (Article 4 ATI); this includes police departments. Therefore, all 17 provincial police departments were asked to provide their Facebook Insights for a period of almost two years, from March 10, 2018, to January 26, 2020. The time frame was chosen based on the Facebook rule that page administrators can export data from two years before the request (Facebook, 2020). Of the 17 provincial police departments, 14 shared their Insights data. One data package was incomplete; therefore, posts from 13 fan pages were chosen for further analysis. In the end, the sample size was 13,963 posts. Based on the literature, we identified 16 main categories and 19 subcategories for classifying a post (Table 3.1). Every category was defined by the researchers. After every member of the research team had coded the same 100 posts, we discussed all the inconsistencies and added necessary details to the definitions created earlier. Every post in the sample was then coded by at least one member of the research team.

Table 3.2 Number of likes given to every police department over the time of research (January 2020)

Provincial police departments	*Likes*
Lubelska Policja	10,367
Lubuska Policja	18,862
Łódzka Policja	13,629
Mazowiecka Policja	6,686
Opolska Policja	5,920
Podkarpacka Policja	5,011
Podlaska Policja	6,804
Pomorska Policja	8,946
Śląska Policja	15,205
Świętokrzyska Policja	5,673
Warmińsko-Mazurska Policja	4,828
Wielkopolska Policja	24,337
Zachodniopomorska Policja	4,006

The researchers also identified the popularity of particular profiles, based on the likes gained by each police department across the data collection period (Table 3.2).

Table 3.2 shows that over this period, one police department's fan page had far more likes than any of the others. This was Wielkopolska Policja, with 24,337 likes; its profile was established in 2015. The least popular profile was that of Zachodniopomorska Policja (set up in 2017); it received only 4,006 likes. Both profiles will be compared with the general results for police Facebook posts to verify if the number of likes is correlated with the number of "funny and cute content" posts.

Results

The first step was to identify all posts uploaded by Polish provincial police departments from the categories included in "funny and cute content" (Table 3.3). The data covers posts uploaded during a period of 22 months between March 10, 2018, and January 26, 2020.

Table 3.3 shows that there were a total of 406 posts coded as "funny and cute content" – less than 3% of all posts. Among "funny and cute content," the most popular were K9 posts; there were 189 of these, 1.35% of the total. Funny Content also made up more than 1% of all posts (158 posts in total). The least popular category was Service Horse; there were only 59 such posts, just 0.42% of all gathered data. The reason for the higher popularity of K9 in comparison to Service Horse posts may be the general number of animals used by Polish police; in 2020, there were over 900 police dogs, but only 54 service horses (Ministry of Internal Affairs and Administration, 2021). Overall, it seems that

Table 3.3 Posts uploaded by Polish police departments within the categories included in "Funny and cute content"

Post type	*Number of posts*	*% of total*
All posts	13,963	100
K9	189	1.35
Service Horse	59	0.42
Funny Content	158	1.13
Funny and cute content (all together)	406	2.90

Table 3.4 Chosen Facebook Insights for the posts uploaded by Polish police departments within the categories included in "Funny and cute content"

Post type	*Number of posts*	*Lifetime post total reach (average)*	*Lifetime engaged users (average)*	*Negative feedback (average)*
All posts	13,963	7,547	774	1
K9	189	7,961	568	1
Service Horse	59	8,053	502	1
Funny Content	158	13,531	1,507	1
Funny and cute content posts (all together)	406	10,144	963	1

publishing "funny and cute content" is not a strategy generally used by Polish police to gather fan-page followers.

The second hypothesis about the engagement activities in "funny and cute content" posts may be evaluated based on the numbers shown in Table 3.4.

Table 3.4 shows that the average number of users who had the page's post appear on their screen (Lifetime Post Total Reach) was 7,547. All posts within "funny and cute content" had greater reach than the average post, with Funny Content being the highest at almost double the average.

As mentioned before, the crucial Facebook Insight is the one that shows user engagement with a post. Engagement is understood as liking the post, sharing it, clicking an element of the post, or commenting on it. It must be highlighted that when it comes to commenting, Facebook does not separate positive from negative opinions; nevertheless, every comment means the content is engaging for the user. While the average engagement in a post was 774, animal posts (K9 and Service Horse) were on a similar, below-average level of engagement (K9 – 568, Service Horse – 502). In contrast, Funny Content posts were much more engaging than other uploaded content (average engagement of 1,507). Together, all the posts from "funny and cute content" generated more engagement than the average post uploaded by the Polish police. Negative Feedback was the same for all categories analyzed in this research.

The next step was to gather the Insight data for the two chosen police departments. The provincial police department with the greatest number of likes was Wielkopolska Policja. In 2020, its fan page had 24,337 likes, and it had reached 52,344 by the time of writing (2023). Table 3.5 shows the number of posts uploaded in the categories of "funny and cute content."

Table 3.5 shows that Wielkopolska Policja uploaded less than one post a day during the research period. Among all posts, more than 3% each were from the categories K9 and Service Horse, which in both cases was more than the average shown in Table 3.3. There was also much more funny content than the average for Polish police departments (4.55% of all posts). In general, funny and cute content covered 11.03% of all posts uploaded by Wielkopolska Policja.

Table 3.6 presents the results of Facebook Insights analysis for Wielkopolska Policja posts categorized as "funny and cute content."

Neither K9, Service Horse, nor Funny Content reached the average Lifetime Post Total Reach for posts uploaded by Wielkopolska Policja (21,827). The same tendency may be observed for the level of engagement. The closest to the average level of 2,504 engaged activities were posts marked as Funny Content, with 2,334 interactions. K9 and Service Horse were well below

Table 3.5 Posts uploaded by Wielkopolska Policja within the categories included in "Funny and cute content"

Post type	*Number of posts*	*% of total*
All posts	571	100
K9	19	3.32
Service Horse	18	3.15
Funny Content	26	4.55
Funny and cute content posts (all together)	63	11.03

Table 3.6 Chosen Facebook Insights for the posts uploaded by Wielkopolska Policja within the categories included in "Funny and cute content"

Post type	*Number of posts uploaded by Wielkopolska Policja*	*Lifetime post total reach (average)*	*Lifetime engaged users (average)*	*Negative feedback (average)*
All posts	571	21,827	2,504	2
K9	19	12,777	902	2
Service Horse	18	16,073	960	2
Funny Content	26	18,670	2,334	2
Funny and cute content posts (all together)	63	16,151	1,509	2

average (K9 – 902 activities, Service Horse – 960 activities). Negative Feedback remained the same in all categories; it was the same as for other categories of posts published by Wielkopolska Policja. Although about 1 in 10 posts by Wielkopolska Policja were coded as "funny and cute content," these posts did not generate the engagement predicted by marketing research. However, it seems that Wielkopolska Policja found other strategies to interest users in its uploaded content.

The second provincial police department chosen for analysis was Zachodniopomorska Policja. Its Facebook profile was established in 2017, and at the time of research it had 4,006 likes. As the profile has since been deleted, there is no information on the number of Zachodniopomorska Policja fan page likes in 2023.

Table 3.7 shows that Zachodniopomorska Policja uploaded 1,580 posts during the research period – more than 2 posts a day. The number of posts, including "funny and cute content," was 31, which was less than 2% of all coded posts. The majority of these (22) were posts with police dogs. However, this was still only 1.39% of all posts published by Zachodniopomorska Policja during the research period. There were almost no posts marked by the research team as Funny Content (only 3).

Table 3.8 presents the results of Facebook Insights for Zachodniopomorska Policja posts categorized as "funny and cute content."

The Lifetime Total Reach for an average post published by Zachodniopomorska Policja was 2,175. The numbers show that posts marked as K9, Service Horse, and Funny Content were more viral than the average post uploaded by Zachodniopomorska Policja. The user engagement in a post was, on average, 216, compared to 283 for K9, 285 for Service Horse, and 287 for Funny Content.

The numbers show that although Zachodniopomorska Policja uploaded a large number of posts, it did not introduce a "funny and cute content" strategy. Still, posts marked as K9, Service Horse, and Funny Content seem to have been a bit more engaging than the average post.

Table 3.7 Posts uploaded by Zachodniopomorska Policja within the categories included in "Funny and cute content"

Post type	*Number of Posts*	*% of total*
All posts	1,580	100
K9	22	1.39
Service Horse	6	0.37
Funny Content	3	0.18
Funny and cute content posts (all together)	31	1.96

Table 3.8 Chosen Facebook Insights for the posts uploaded by Zachodniopomorska Policja within the categories included in "Funny and cute content"

Post type	*Number of posts uploaded by Zachodniopomorska Policja*	*Lifetime Post Total Reach (average)*	*Lifetime Engaged Users (average)*	*Negative Feedback (average)*
All posts	1,580	2,175	216	0
K9	22	2,513	283	0
Service Horse	6	3,634	285	1
Funny Content	3	4,123	287	1
Funny and cute content posts (all together)	31	2,886	284	0

Discussion and conclusion

This study has focused on strategies that can be used to get public attention for Polish provincial police departments' fan pages on Facebook. While gathering the data for analyzing the social media activity of Polish police departments, it was found that there are no detailed instructions for them on how to maintain an official Facebook profile. In the end, the uploaded content depends on the knowledge and personal experience of the police officers responsible for social media in each particular unit. The main goal of every Facebook profile administrator should be to get followers. The case is, however, more complicated when it comes to public entities whose task is serving the community. Nevertheless, more visibility may be helpful in achieving this aim.

This accords with the "new visibility" theory introduced by Thompson (2005), who claimed that new ways of communicating (e.g., video sharing in digital space) provide opportunities to easily express one's aims. However, as Goldsmith (2010) has noted, in the police context, this may also be a threat to forces' image, as officers' misconduct may be exposed to the public. Therefore, the police should identify a proper social media strategy; this may be a chance to gain more legitimacy and build trust in the community (Kudla & Parnaby, 2018). Gathering a broader audience may facilitate investigating crimes by, for example, searching for witnesses or identifying suspects. It may also help to prevent crime by spreading social campaigns and sharing prevention tips. Performing a public service on social media is, however, impossible when people are not following the fan page. Therefore, police units should look for the best strategy to combine their public obligations with uploading interesting content for potential audiences. Although researchers have tried to identify what social media content gets the greatest interest among users (e.g., Lieberman et al., 2013; Hu et al., 2018), there is no worldwide accepted strategy on how police departments should maintain their social media profiles. Police units may, however, look for other law enforcement agencies that are successfully using social media. Although there is no agreement on how to define success in maintaining police units' Facebook profiles, one of the crucial elements is spreading the content to the greatest number of users. One strategy that fulfills this definition is the "meme strategy" used by NSWP in Australia. Building an audience by using funny content was, in this case, helpful for disseminating other important police information (Wood, 2020b). Engagement in funny content was also emphasized by Crilley and Pears (2021), who noted that jokes and pop culture references in CIA Twitter posts were popular among social media users. Other authors, however, have stressed that using humor on social media may be dangerous for the legitimacy of an institution when "public authorities create popularity around themselves on grounds other than their performance of primary duties" (Rasmussen, 2017).

The general rule on how social media algorithms work, and the experience of Australian police, may indicate that content including animals and funny forms are interesting for the audience (Wood, 2020a). The aim of this chapter was to verify if the Polish police are using the same strategy. Taking into account legal, social, and cultural differences, I adapted Wood's "meme strategy" to a more suitable "funny and cute content" strategy. The analysis shows that the first hypothesis – *Polish police will use funny and cute content to increase the popularity of their Facebook profiles* – was partially falsified. It turns out that posts included in a "funny and cute content" strategy are not often published by provincial police departments in Poland. This hypothesis was also checked separately for two provincial police departments: the one with the highest number of likes and the one with the lowest number of likes over the time of research. Both were identified as units where police dogs and service horses are used. The most popular unit used more "funny and cute content" in its posts than the least popular unit.

The second hypothesis – *Posts belonging to "funny and cute content" categories will have more engagement activities than other posts* – was only partially true. Overall, the analyzed posts generated more engagement than the average post published by a provincial police department. However, out of K9, Service Horse, and Funny Content, only the last encouraged users to be more active; engagement almost doubled for Funny Content posts. Bear in mind that engagement does not always mean positive interaction with the content: a published post may trigger both positive and negative comments. This was not the subject of in-depth research in this analysis; it should, however, be analyzed further. If funny content causes more negative than positive comments, police departments should reconsider publishing such posts. The higher engagement for Funny Content was also visible for the most and least popular provincial police departments. However, for the most popular department, animal content (K9, Service Horse) was less engaging than other posts.

Nowadays, there are more and more users of social media; not only private companies but also public entities must find ways to reach them by publishing the appropriate content. "Appropriate," however, might not mean the same thing for institutions such as police forces as it does for commercial brands. Nevertheless, police must find a publishing strategy to make their social media profiles viral and engaging. As there is no one ideal strategy, every police department must independently decide how to maintain a social media profile to gather followers. This should be based on their national sociocultural background (e.g., the level of trust in the police) and organizational structures. However, the most important but also the most difficult issue seems to be finding the right balance between the informal social media style and the legitimacy of the institution.

Reference list

Act of 6 September 2001 on Access to Information Act (ATI). Retrieved April 12, 2023, from https://isap.sejm.gov.pl/isap.nsf/download.xsp/WDU20011121198/U/D20011198Lj.pdf

Bayerl, S., Jacobs, G., & Horton, K. (2017). Ignoring, tolerating or embracing? Social media use in European police forces. *European Law Enforcement Research Bulletin*, (2), 295–308.

Bullock, K. (2018). The police use of social media: Transformation or normalisation? Social policy and society. *A Journal of the Social Policy Association, 17*(2), 245–258.

Crilley, R., & Pears, L. (2021). "No, we don't know where Tupac is": Critical intelligence studies and the CIA on social media. *Intelligence and National Security*, *36*(4), 599–614.

Facebook. (2020). *How do I export my Facebook page's insights data?* Retrieved September 21, 2023, from www.facebook.com/help/972879969525875

Fb NSW Police Force. (2022). https://www.facebook.com/nswpoliceforce/

Fb Wielkopolska Policja. (2023). https://www.facebook.com/PolicjaWlkp/?locale=pl_PL

Goldsmith, A. (2010). Policing's new visibility. *The British Journal of Criminology*, *50*(5), 914–934.

How Facebook Distributes Content. (2022). Retrieved April 12, 2023, from www.facebook.com/business/help/718033381901819?id=208060977200861

Hu, X., Rodgers, K., & Lovrich, N. P. (2018). "We are more than crime fighters": Social media images of police departments. *Police Quarterly*, *21*(4), 544–572.

IACP Law Enforcement Policy Center. (2019). *Social media: Considerations*. Retrieved April 12, 2023, from www.theiacp.org/sites/default/files/2019-05/Social%20Media%20Considerations%20-%202019.pdf

Kudla, D., & Parnaby, P. (2018). To serve and to Tweet: An examination of police-related Twitter activity in Toronto. *Social Media + Society*, *4*(3), 1–13.

Liam, R. (2022). The dynamic nature of police legitimacy on social media. *Policing and Society, 32*(7), 817–831.

Lieberman, J. D., Koetzle, D., & Sakiyama, M. (2013). Police departments' use of Facebook: Patterns and policy issues. *Police Quarterly*, *16*(4), 438–462.

Livingstone, R. M. (2022). Public relations and public service: Police departments on Facebook. *International Journal of Research and Policy, 32*(5), 598–610.

Oglesby-Neal, A., & Warnberg, C. (2019, February). *Law enforcement social media policies, report*. Urban Institute.

Peters, B. (2019). *Facebook marketing in 2019: A study of 777M Facebook posts*. Retrieved April 12, 2023, from https://buffer.com/resources/facebook-marketing-2019/

Ministry of Internal Affairs and Administration *Psy i konie w służbach MSWiA* (2021). Retrieved April 12, 2023, from www.gov.pl/web/mswia/psy-i-konie-w-sluzbach-mswia

Rasmussen, J. (2017). "Welcome to Twitter, @CIA. Better late than never": Communication professionals' views of social media humour and implications for organizational identity. *Discourse & Communication, 11*(1), 89–110.

Statista. (2022a). *Number of internet and social media users worldwide as of January 2023*. Retrieved April 12, 2023, from www.statista.com/statistics/617136/digital-population-worldwide/

Statista. (2022b). *Number of social media users worldwide from 2017 to 2027*. Retrieved April 12, 2023, from www.statista.com/statistics/278414/number-of-worldwide-social-network-users/

Statista. (2022c). *Share of adults who use social media as a source of news in selected countries worldwide as of February 2022*. Retrieved April 12, 2023, from www.statista.com/statistics/718019/social-media-news-source/

Thompson, J. B. (2005). The new visibility. *Theory, Culture & Society, 22*(6), 31–51.

Waszkiewicz, P., Tomaszewska-Michalak, M., Stromczyński, B., & Rabczuk, S. (2021). Czy wielkopolska policja umie w internety? Analiza strategii komunikacyjnej KWP w Poznaniu na portalu Facebook. In P. Waszkiewicz (Ed.), *Media społecznościowe w pracy organów ścigania* (pp. 61–81). Instytut Nauk Prawnych PAN.

Wood, M. A. (2020a). Policing's "meme strategy": Understanding the rise of police social media engagement work. *Current Issues in Criminal Justice, 32*(1), 40–58.

Wood, M. A. (2020b). Memetic copaganda: Understanding the humorous turn in police image work. *Crime, Media, Culture: An International Journal, 17*(3), 305–326.

4 We are still here – police activity on social media during the COVID-19 pandemic

Błażej Stromczyński

Introduction

"One of the men who was quarantined had a birthday today. Policewomen from Kalisz who visited him today surprised him – Happy Birthday was sung, a beautiful banner was presented, and a big round of applause for the jubilarian was given. We also join the wishes. #stayathome" (Wielkopolska Policja, 2020a). This video was posted by a Facebook user and later reposted on the profile of the regional police department (RPD) of the Wielkopolskie voivodeship ("Wielkopolska Policja") on April 9, 2020. The post was seen by 30,184 users, and 4,399 unique users engaged in some way with the publication. Ten days before, on March 31, 2020, the Polish government had imposed a strict stay-at-home policy for the period April 1–11. For non-compliant actions, the regulations included criminal sanctions typical for misdemeanors, such as reprimands or fines.

Later, on April 20, 2020, the profile of Wielkopolska Policja announced that on the following day, the full functionality of the district police station in Krotoszyn would be restored; 65 police officers would report on duty, while the remaining 26 were still being treated for COVID-19 infection. The station had been closed for two weeks (Wielkopolska Policja, 2020b).

Both posts showed the new reality of COVID-19 lockdowns, to which all institutions, including law enforcement agencies, had to adjust. Instead of focusing primarily on their typical tasks, such as crime investigation, the emphasis shifted more toward protecting public order and safety, including the enforcement of social distancing and quarantine regulations.

Crime rates and structure during extraordinary events

The first case of COVID-19 in Poland was reported on March 4, 2020 (Ministerstwo Zdrowia, 2020). Over three years later, on July 1, 2023, the epidemic emergency was lifted. Poland and the entire world had been fighting a virus that brought long-unseen suffering and casualties. As of October 4, 2023, 771,151,224 confirmed cases of COVID-19, including 6,960,783 deaths, had been reported to the WHO (WHO, 2023). The pandemic changed people's

DOI: 10.4324/9781032680194-4
This chapter has been made available under a CC-BY-NC 4.0 license.

realities and had a great impact on almost all aspects of life. It also resulted in a variety of crimes being committed, as well as deep changes in the activities of public bodies, including law enforcement agencies.

A significant number of academics have conducted research on criminality during the COVID-19 era. A September 2021 data summary of criminological research projects around the world enumerated 68 studies on various subjects such as human trafficking and child abuse, domestic violence, and prison living conditions (Ribeiro et al., 2021). A number of criminological studies of COVID-19 were based on the foundation that extraordinary incidents such as "natural disasters, terrorist attacks, riots and pandemics" can cause changes in the criminal behavior observed in society (Hodgkinson & Andresen, 2020, p. 1). Classical criminology theories could be considered relevant for analyzing crime rate changes during the pandemic.

The classic theory of social altruism – defined as "the willingness of communities to commit, distinct from the beneficence of the state, scarce resources to aid and comfort their members" (Chamlin & Cochran, 1997, p. 210) – was confirmed in the COVID-19 pandemic by Grimalda et al. (2021), whose research showed that "people donated a significant amount of resources [for relief efforts] in a situation of existential threat" (p. 9). In crime, this theory could be used to predict a greater willingness of people to help each other rather than take advantage of other community members during extreme events, resulting in the crime rate remaining steady or falling. Such an occurrence was demonstrated by Zahran et al. (2009) in a study conducted in Florida.

In social disorganization theory, the weakening of social relations caused by extraordinary events will cause a rise in the crime rate. This was indicated, for example, in a study by Sampson and Groves, who stated that "communities characterized by sparse friendship networks, unsupervised teenage peer groups, and low organizational participation had disproportionately high rates of crime and delinquency" (Sampson & Groves, 1989, p. 799). The COVID-19 pandemic could easily be characterized as an extraordinary event that might break many relations between community members.

According to routine activity theory (RAT) proposed by Cohen and Felson, three key elements of crime need to occur together: a motivated offender, a suitable target, and the absence of capable guardians against a violation (Cohen & Felson, 1979, p. 589). Hodgkinson and Andresen (2020, p. 2) argue that in line with RAT, during extraordinary times, the rates of some crimes will increase while others fall; for example, there will be fewer opportunities for burglaries, as more people will stay at home.

Studies have shown that the last theory prevailed in the COVID-19 era. The results of an initial analysis of the relationship between the pandemic and crime, conducted by Ashby (2020b),

> found no significant changes in the frequency of serious assaults either in public or in residences (contrary to concerns among practitioners and policy

> makers), reductions in residential burglary in some (but not all) cities, little change in nonresidential burglary (except in Minneapolis), decreases in thefts from vehicles in some cities, and diverging patterns of thefts of vehicles.
>
> (p. 15)

It has been reported that domestic violence, burglary, and vehicle theft crimes dropped significantly during the stay-at-home policy in Mexico (Balmori de la Miyar et al., 2021). In Detroit, the burglary rate dropped; meanwhile, burglaries shifted from residential neighborhoods to areas where residential properties were significantly intermingled with nonresidential land uses (Felson et al., 2020, pp. 4–5). An analysis of crime rates in 27 cities within 23 countries showed an "overall drop in police-recorded crime of 37%" (Nivette et al., 2021, p. 873). However, the number of cyber-dependent and cyber-related crimes increased (Gryszczyńska, 2021, p. 1). Media reports suggested that the number of cybercrimes registered by the FBI's Cyber Division increased three- or fourfold in April 2020 (Miller, 2020).

Academics have also discussed the impact of the pandemic on police operations. These studies have focused mainly on areas such as changes in calls for service (CFS) (Ashby, 2020a), the impact of the pandemic on the mental health of police officers (Drew & Martin, 2020), and changes in typical police activities and police organization caused by COVID-19 (Nielson et al., 2022; Maskály et al., 2021).

The first field covers changes in requests for help by citizens during extraordinary events such as pandemics. Scholars have focused on factors such as the absence of a significant number of officers due to illness; the emergence of new types of police activities, such as enforcing stay-at-home orders, which heavily burdened police officers' schedules; and the frequency or seriousness of incidents reported by citizens (Ashby, 2020a, p. 1055). In the last area, Ashby studied data calls from 10 of the 100 largest cities in the United States. The call data from January 1, 2016, to January 19, 2020, were used as a ground to establish the "baseline frequency of calls that would be expected in the absence of the pandemic" (p. 1057). This was used to set up a forecast of call structure for January–May 2020, which was then compared with the actual data for that period. In March 2020, when remote learning and strict stay-at-home orders were introduced, the number of calls dropped slightly compared to the projection (Ashby, 2020a, p. 1069). The slight reduction in calls for service during lockdowns has been confirmed in studies of Los Angeles and Indianapolis (Mohler et al., 2020) and Los Angeles only (Campedelli et al., 2021).

The second field is mental health and the impact of COVID-19 on police officers' well-being. A survey and interviews of Hampshire Constabulary police officers and staff by Newiss et al. (2022) showed that almost half of the surveyed police officers "suffered increased anxiety and one quarter an adverse impact on their health" (p. 103). Stogner et al. (2020, p. 724) indicated that COVID-19-related stress could cause reduced police productivity and an increase in misconduct incidents. In Poland, Andraszak (2020) researched police officers' approaches to their tasks via a quantitative study of 184 respondents, conducted in June 2020. This showed that the work engagement of police officers dropped very slightly from 3.98 to 3.80 on a five-point scale (pp. 36–37). The research was conducted after the first lockdown; the results might have been significantly different during the next peaks of coronavirus restrictions, especially since officers were placed under more and more stress factors such as "compassion fatigue and moral suffering" arising from being the first responders in many death-related incidents (Mehdizadeh & Kamkar, 2020, p. 43).

The third field is changes in typical police activities and organizations caused by COVID-19. Maskály et al. (2021) conducted a questionnaire survey on 26 potential police organizational changes arising from COVID-19 in areas such as crime suppression strategies, crime prevention strategies, reactive policing, and COVID-19-related policing (pp. 273–274). In 2020, the representatives of police services of member states of the United Nations Office on Drugs and Crime and police professional organizations evaluated potential changes on a five-point scale from "no change" to "completely changed." In problem-solving and community-policing activities (the areas most related to the use of social media by law enforcement agencies), 83.3% of the participants indicated substantial changes (some change – 54.1%; mostly changed – 16.7%; totally changed – 12.5%). Only 16.7% indicated no change (12.5%) or only slight changes (4.2%) (Maskály et al., 2021, p. 274).

In Poland, lockdowns saw the introduction of a number of restrictions, such as a ban on public gatherings, obligatory mask wearing, and the closure of entertainment facilities (gyms, swimming pools, clubs, dance clubs, fitness clubs, museums, libraries, cinemas, hotels), as well as beaches and forests (Związek Przedsiębiorców i Pracodawców, 2021). To enforce these regulations, the police had to increase their number of preventive actions. According to data presented by Jarczewski (2022, p. 249), by April 6, 2021, over 3.6 million inspections of entertainment facilities had been conducted. The new police task was verification of compliance with quarantine rules by people with COVID-19, who were obliged to stay at home for periods related to their sickness. As of April 6, 2021, the Police had conducted over 63 million controls (Jarczewski, 2022, p. 250). This increased police activity affected the number of misdemeanor proceedings – by April 19, 2021, over 600,000 cases had concluded by imposing fines or submitting motions for fines to the court (Jarczewski, 2022, p. 251). The scale of fines might have been much higher if the police had not used punitive measures of an educational nature, such as instructions and warnings. Between April 16 and May 31, 2020, 69% of controls ended in such non-fine measures (Commissioner for Human Rights, 2020).

Police use of social media for community policing during the pandemic

Research conducted by Lum, Maupin, and Stoltz showed that during the COVID-19 pandemic, 73% of responding agencies located in the United States and Canada "had adopted policies to reduce or limit community-oriented policing activities" (Lum et al., 2020, p. 2). Nielson et al. (2022) found that in Houston, Texas, officers made more self-initiated patrols, which could be seen as strengthening proactive police actions. However, those patrols were enforcing unpopular regulations (stay at home, mask wearing, etc.); therefore, the results might have been the opposite of those originally intended in community policing. As offline contact with citizens grew more difficult, online presence and activity on social media became effective methods for proactive policing.

The objectives of social media use by law enforcement agencies during the pandemic were not totally different from those in ordinary times. Social media could be used for:

- Informing the community about current regulations and safety guidelines.
- Counteracting disinformation and providing links to trusted sources of information (Volkmer, 2021, p. 8).
- Providing educational content and promoting vaccination.
- Building a positive image of the police and their operations (as presented in the introduction).

So far, the use of social media by police during the pandemic has been insufficiently researched; only a few studies have been undertaken. The interviews conducted by Ralph et al. (2022) showed that police online presence could remind community members that "we [police] are still working; we are still going out and doing drugs warrants and things like that" (p. 769). Moreover, online meetings could reach groups not included en masse in offline activities, for example the younger generation. Social media activity could also be more efficient in terms of the ratio of time to audience numbers (Ralph et al., 2022, pp. 768–769). Another aspect highlighted by interviewees was the reposting of COVID-19-related publications from central authorities' profiles, as regulations were changing rapidly, and it was difficult for police officers to create timely and precise content. Finally, the switch from COVID-19-related content to other content was very quick after lockdowns had ended. This was caused by general public fatigue with the subject, negative comments on COVID-19-related posts, and the greater number of offline community policing activities that became available (Ralph et al., 2022, pp. 772–773).

Hu et al. (2022) studied COVID-19-related posts published on police profiles and coded them into five major groups. The sample was collected in September 2020 and included over 2,400 posts from 14 police agencies published over a 4-month period. They compared the results of previous research (a sample starting in 2014) to the COVID-19-related content. The analysis of the 2020 sample showed that "exclusively COVID-19 content represented but a small proportion of overall posts during the early pandemic period" (p. 119). Moreover, police used other agencies' publications as sources of information about the pandemic.

While the objective of police social media use during the pandemic has been clearly defined, and its content has been studied up to a point, the public's perception of it remains largely unexplored. This area warrants particular attention, especially considering the aversion many people had to COVID-19 countermeasures. Obligations like wearing masks, the no-gathering policy, and the introduction of vaccines could all have negatively influenced the public's reaction to police content.

Study

This study examines the use of social media by the Polish police during the COVID-19 pandemic; the research questions focus on the Polish police's approach to COVID-19-related content and their publication strategy. The study also compares publications made in ordinary and extraordinary (pandemic, crisis) times. The following hypotheses will be tested:

H1: *The daily number of posts will be greater in the COVID-19 period than in the pre-COVID-19 period.*

Many community policing activities were moved onto the social media profiles of RPDs; therefore, the total number of posts published in the COVID-19 period should be greater than in the pre-COVID period.

H2: *COVID-19-related posts will not be posted after pandemic peaks (such as lockdowns and more severe limitations); other types of content will be published instead.*

This practice was indicated by several English interviewees.

H3: *COVID-19-related posts will have greater total reach and total engagement than typical publications posted by RPDs in the same period.*

Police social media profiles should be used as sources of information or for counteracting disinformation; therefore, COVID-19-related posts should generate more engagement among users.

H4: *Posts reposting information on newly introduced restrictions from other authorities' profiles will be more common than original restrictions information content created by RPDs.*

Due to rapid changes in legislation regarding COVID-19 protective measures, the Polish police will not use their resources to adapt and present legal regulations to be understandable to the public. Content already prepared by appropriate entities will be reposted instead.

Method

To verify the hypotheses, Facebook posts published by Polish RPDs were analyzed quantitatively and qualitatively. Possible methods for extraction of post data include manual analysis, data scraping (generally forbidden by Facebook's regulations), and collecting data from profile administrators (Waszkiewicz et al., 2023). In this study, the Facebook Insights data were collected from RPD profiles' administrators by an Access to Information request that was sent to all 17 RPDs operating within Poland. The obtained data were split into two periods: March 10, 2018, to January 25, 2020 (pre-COVID-19 data/sample), and January 26, 2020, to March 26, 2021 (COVID-19 data/sample). The starting date for the COVID-19 data was set in January 2020, even though the first confirmed case in Poland was not identified until March. However, on January 26, cases of coronavirus had already been spotted outside China – for example, in Japan (3), the United States (3), and France (3) (Berlinger, 2020) – and European governments had started making preparations for border closures. On January 24, 2020, the biggest airport in Poland introduced special procedures for passengers coming from China (Wirus z Chin, 2020). The end date of COVID-19 data was set in March 2021, just when the number of cases of the Alpha coronavirus mutation started to rise, and another lockdown was introduced by the government (Portal Gov.pl, 2021).

Data eligible for further analysis were provided by 13 RPDs for the pre-COVID-19 sample and 11 RPDs for the COVID-19 sample. The other RPDs either did not consider the data to be public information or did not provide sufficient data for review and analysis (parts of the data were missing). Due to the different lengths of each period (686 days for the pre-COVID-19 data, 425 for the COVID-19 data), the number of analyzed posts also differed – there were 13,947 posts in the first period and 8,672 in the second.

Using the coding areas from previous research (Waszkiewicz et al., 2021, pp. 43–44), every pre-COVID-19 post was reviewed and categorized into one of 6 groups and 29 subgroups, and the numerical data from all RPDs were assembled into one table. For the COVID-19 posts, publications related to the pandemic were identified using keywords relevant to COVID-19. From this selection, 993 posts were manually reviewed, and 811 were finally recognized as COVID-19-related posts. The latter content was grouped into the 9 categories presented in Table 4.1.

Table 4.1 Categories of COVID-19-related publications

#	*Category*	*Description*
1	Regulations	Posts regarding legal regulations introduced for counteracting COVID-19; the content was treated as locally created if there was no link or the link led to the RPD's website; if the link led to another Polish police or other state authority website, the content was considered as centrally created.
2	Organizational changes	Content related to changes in police stations such as visits limitation or introducing crimes reporting by email as well as changes in officers' behavior during interventions.
3	Cases	Publications regarding interventions, fines, and arrests related to non-compliance to COVID-19 regulations; the category included other crimes with COVID-19 included in the crime description (e.g. cyber fraud case with use of COVID-19 adapted scenario).
4	Tips – crime prevention	Advice for victimization prevention in case of frauds with the use of COVID-19 reality; the category also included warnings on fake news.
5	Tips – COVID-19 health and safety	Advices how to limit the transmission of COVID-19; the category included public appeals to #stayathome; provides true information about health measures and appeals to get vaccinated at a later stage of COVID-19 pandemic.
6	Police in action	Publications regarding any activities of police officers during COVID-19, especially related to new tasks caused by COVID-19, such as enforcing stay-at-home orders, entertainment facilities inspections, and handing out masks.
7	Plasma/blood donation	Information about officers donating blood/plasma as well as public appeals for such action.
8	Stay-at-home mobile application	Public appeals for using state developed mobile application (ProteGo Safe) that facilitated and improved the mandatory quarantine at home.
9	Other	State ceremonies, funny posts, providing the personal protective equipment to the police, expression of gratitude by citizens, etc.

Results

Given that the samples varied in terms of the number of days and the number of RPDs, the most comparable metric was the average number of posts published by each individual RPD. The data analysis revealed that each RPD published an average of 1.56 posts per day in the pre-COVID-19 sample. This increased to 1.85 in the COVID-19 sample, marking an 18.34% growth in publications during the pandemic. Therefore, H1 was confirmed.

The number of COVID-19 posts decreased significantly shortly after the first lockdown's restrictions started to be lifted. In Poland, this was conducted in stages: on April 20, 2020, visits to forests were allowed; on May 4, malls and hotels were reopened; entertainment facilities followed on May 18. Posts on COVID-19 dropped significantly from 244 in March and 265 in April to 67 in May and only 19 in June. In the following months, COVID-19-related content was identified in fewer than 50 posts. H2 was, therefore, confirmed. The monthly distribution of COVID-19-related posts was compared to all posts published in both samples. The analysis did not show a significant correlation between the given month and the number of posts published (especially in March and April) in either sample (Graphs 4.1 and 4.2).

It stands to reason that social media users would seek information about the pandemic on state-controlled profiles. RPDs' Facebook profiles could be considered as reliable sources of information about upcoming regulations and restrictions already introduced. Therefore, their posts about COVID-19 might have greater total reach and engagement than typical posts by RPDs in the same period. The analysis showed that the total average reach for COVID-19 content was 31,045.50, while the average engagement was 3,654.99. Both values were significantly higher than for typical posts from the COVID-19 sample (average reach 19,742.56; engagement 1,597.53). Moreover, both results were significantly greater than the average pre-COVID-19 post (reach 7,547.24; engagement 774.36). H3 was, therefore, confirmed.

The dynamics of changes related to COVID-19 were very rapid, and often the legislative actions did not follow the current pandemic reality. Nevertheless, a great many new restrictions were introduced (discussion of the legal grounds and appropriateness of the methods of introducing them is outside the scope of this chapter). With so many legal updates and difficulties in interpreting them, it was easier for RPDs to base their posts on more precise governmental sources – both profiles and websites. The study showed that out of 47 posts defined as Regulations, 57.45% were reposted or directed straight to governmental websites, with thorough information on newly introduced rules. The remaining 42.55% of posts within the Regulations group were created locally and directed to the websites of RPDs. H4 was confirmed.

Discussion

The quantitative analysis revealed that most posts related to COVID-19 concerned police action (29.3%) and cases (21.3%). This approach was in line with trends observed in other countries – in their COVID-19-related content, police showed that they were still present and enforcing new laws, even under pandemic circumstances. Moreover, many of the restrictions were questioned and

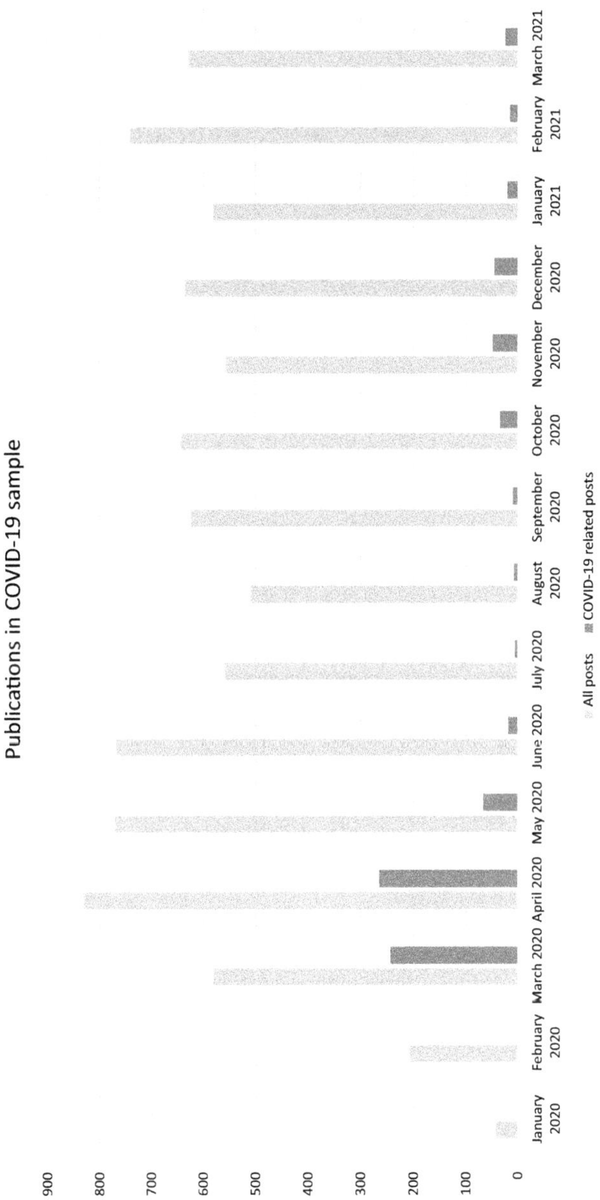

Graph 4.1 Number of monthly publications in the COVID-19 sample

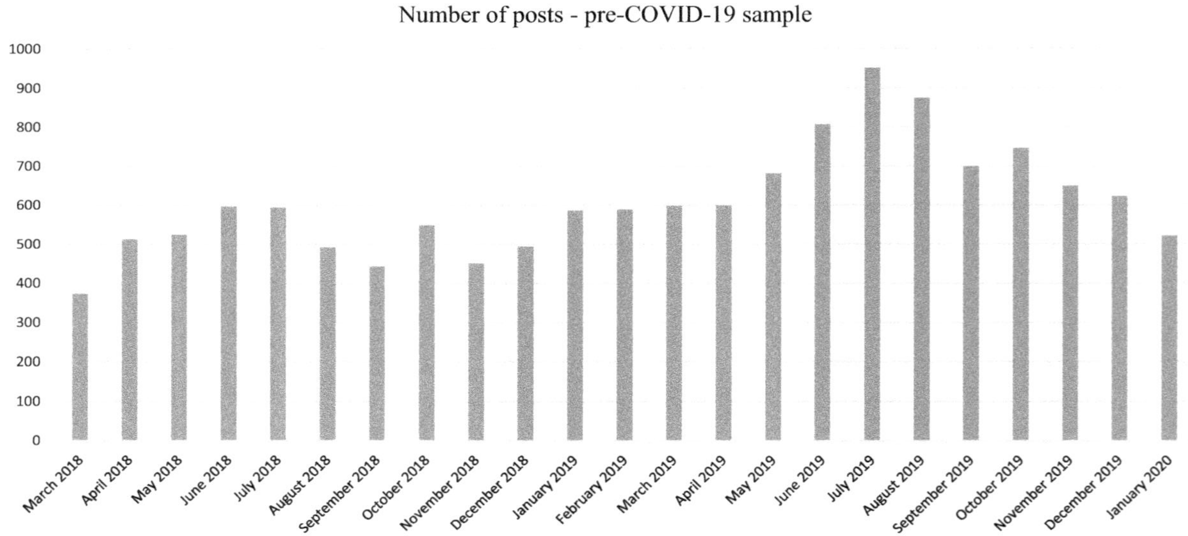

Graph 4.2 Number of monthly publications in the pre-COVID sample

Table 4.2 Results of the COVID-19 sample analysis

Category	*Number of posts*	*Percentage of COVID-19 posts*	*Average lifetime post total reach*	*Average lifetime engaged users*
Cases	173	21.3%	11603.03	1406.73
Organizational changes	26	3.2%	65083.69	5197.65
Other	122	15.0%	75790.20	13507.48
Plasma/blood donation	48	5.9%	39598.15	1901.75
Police in action	238	29.3%	29306.29	2462.18
Regulations	47	5.8%	8535.43	888.30
Stay at home mobile application	30	3.7%	8652.03	720.20
Tips – COVID-19 health & safety	79	9.7%	28685.30	2031.19
Tips – crime prevention	48	5.9%	8948.44	764.19
Total	*811*	*100.0%*	*31045.50*	*3654.99*

challenged by citizens; therefore, police-in-action posts could also be perceived as image-building content (PR). This was much needed: the image of the Polish police took another hit in October and November 2020 as police brutality was observed in massive strikes against anti-abortion laws (Starzewski, 2020).

On the other hand, posts about regulations (5.8%) and organizational changes (3.2%) were rare. However, the latter category generated the second-highest average total reach: 65,083.69 users. The most engaging posts were in the Other category, with 13,507.48 people clicking anywhere in the post. The smallest average total reach was for posts dealing with regulations: 8,535.43. The full results of average reach and user engagement are presented in Table 4.2.

The greatest reach was generated by posts published by Wielkopolska Policja, the profile with the greatest number of followers in 2021 (Waszkiewicz et al., 2021, p. 67), and the Warsaw Metropolitan Police Department (KSP). The top five posts, in terms of reach, displayed characteristics typical of viral content: all were videos, with three of them adopting a humorous tone. Moreover, all these posts were published between March 25 and April 8, 2020 – when the first lockdown was introduced, and the numbers of deaths and quarantines were spiking for the first time, as presented in Graph 4.3 (Portal Gov.pl, 2022).

Conclusions

This study focused on social media content published by Polish RPDs during the first year of the COVID-19 pandemic. The results were compared with data from a pre-COVID-19 sample. Most of the posts related to COVID-19

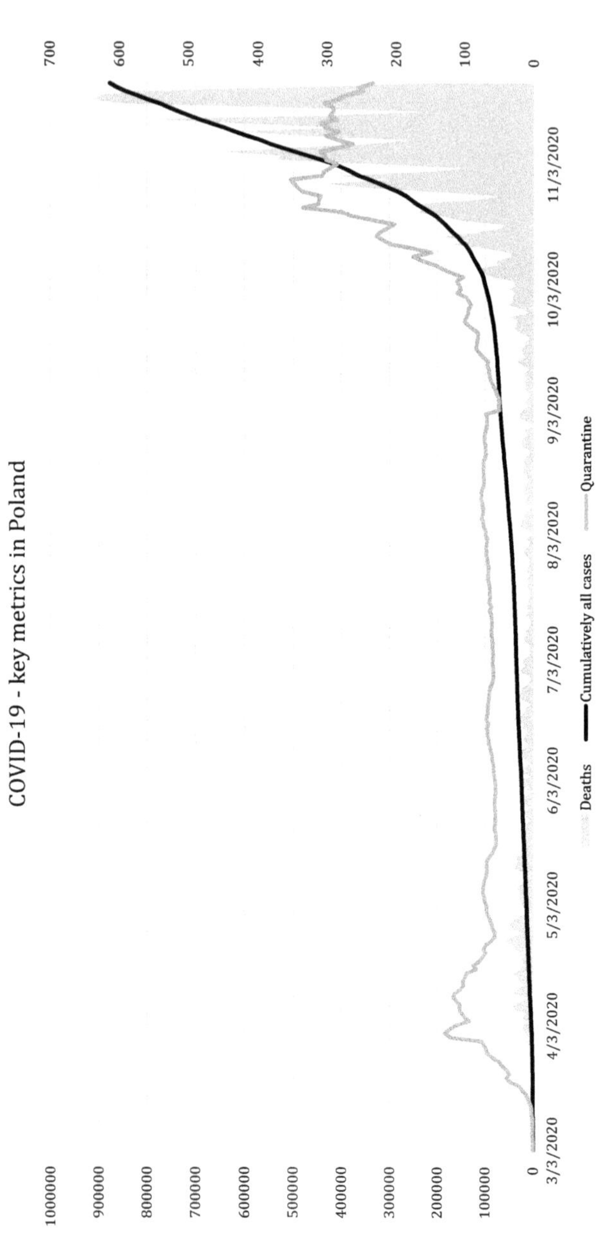

Graph 4.3 Number of deaths and quarantines between March and November 2020

(9.35% of all posts in the COVID-19 sample) were made between March and May 2020, when the first peak of coronavirus hit Poland. The content published by RPDs on their Facebook profiles varied in subject; however, next to ordinary PR posts, RPDs appealed to people to stay at home and, later, to get vaccinated. They also published general tips for not getting sick with COVID-19, such as basic information about washing hands.

Before COVID-19 started, remote work was available for several groups of employees, such as IT professionals. When lockdowns were introduced, a large proportion of office employees had to start working remotely. Due to the unique character of police operations, such standards could not be introduced fully in police stations. However, in March 2020, the Warsaw Metropolitan Police Department stated that police officers could be contacted via the Moja Komenda application or by email (Komenda Stołeczna Policji, 2020). The new method of communication and crime reporting by email was also mentioned in interviews with police officers conducted by Ostaszewski (Ostaszewski et al., 2021, p. 78). Such changes, next to the use of social media by police, should be considered as part of the digitalization of the formation. The organizational changes in police departments' day-to-day operations forced by the pandemic (i.e., contact via email) were also announced on RPDs' social media profiles.

During the rise of COVID-19, new types of fraud based on pandemic themes were identified. According to CERT Polska (the first Polish computer emergency response team operating within the Research and Academic Computer Network – NASK), the number of IT security incidents between January 1 and June 30, 2020, was almost 50% more than in the same period in 2019 (Ostaszewski et al., 2021, p. 53). As people's routine activity shifted from the physical to the digital environment, studies found that "reports of cyber-dependent crime and online fraud have increased during the COVID-19 outbreak, and rates of cybercrimes have been particularly high during months with the strictest lockdown policies" (Buil-Gil et al., 2021, p. 55). The activities of Polish police on social media could be seen as a desirable response to such changes in the structure and rates of crime: RPDs tried to warn the public about such methods and published a number of posts describing the most popular practices of criminals and attack vectors. Moreover, the growth in frequency of posting in the COVID-19 sample could be seen as in line with statements by English police officers: asserting the police's presence even though their activities had shifted. Viewed through the RAT approach, police activity on social media reassured the public that capable guardians were still there and still present to prevent crime rates from increasing.

Additionally, the analysis conducted in this chapter has confirmed the view of Hu et al. (2022) that nowadays, social media is another tool used by the police next to more traditional ways of performing their duties. Its usefulness was especially visible in a time of crisis, when social media users were more interested in COVID-19-related content on RPDs' profiles than in other posts. Such utilization of social media should be considered valuable in any future crises.

Finally, although police activity and content published on social media can assist in achieving various objectives, further research is warranted on public perception, as studied inter alia through comments, sentiment analysis, and potential changes in the public image of the police. If communication with communities and the public through social media proves insufficient, other methods should be considered.

References

Andraszak, N. (2020). Zaangażowanie policjantów w czasie kryzysu: jak pandemia COVID-19 zmieniła pracę funkcjonariuszy Policji? *e-Mentor*, *85*(2020), 32–40.

Ashby, M. P. J. (2020a). Changes in police calls for service during the early months of the 2020 coronavirus pandemic. *Policing: A Journal of Policy and Practice, 14*, 1054–1072. https://doi.org/10.1093/police/paaa037

Ashby, M. P. J. (2020b). Initial evidence on the relationship between the coronavirus pandemic and crime in the United States. *Crime Science*, *9*(1), 6. https://doi.org/10.1186/s40163-020-00117-6

Balmori de la Miyar, J. R., Hoehn-Velasco, L., & Silverio-Murillo, A. (2021). Druglords don't stay at home: COVID-19 pandemic and crime patterns in Mexico City. *Journal of Criminal Justice*, *72*, 101745. https://doi.org/10.1016/j.jcrimjus.2020.101745

Berlinger, J., McKeehan, B., & John, T. (2020). January 26 coronavirus news [WWW document]. *CNN*. Retrieved July 3, 2023, from www.cnn.com/asia/live-news/coronavirus-outbreak-hnk-intl-01-26-20/index.html

Buil-Gil, D., Miró-Llinares, F., Moneva, A., Kemp, S., & Díaz-Castaño, N. (2021). Cybercrime and shifts in opportunities during COVID-19: A preliminary analysis in the UK. *European Societies*, *23*(sup1), S47–S59. https://doi.org/10.1080/14616696.2020.1804973

Campedelli, G. M., Aziani, A., & Favarin, S. (2021). Exploring the effects of COVID-19 containment policies on crime: An empirical analysis of the short-term aftermath in Los Angeles. *American Journal of Criminal Justice*, *46*, 704–727. https://doi.org/10.1007/s12103-020-09578-6

Chamlin, M. B., & Cochran, J. K. (1997). Social altruism and crime*. *Criminology*, *35*(2), 203–226. https://doi.org/10.1111/j.1745-9125.1997.tb00875.x

Cohen, L. E., & Felson, M. (1979). Social change and crime rate trends: A routine activity approach. *American Sociological Review*, *44*(4), 588–608. https://doi.org/10.2307/2094589

Commissioner for Human Rights, V.7018.398.2020.GH – request of May 21, 2020.

Drew, J. M., & Martin, S. (2020). Mental health and well-being of police in a health pandemic: Critical issues for police leaders in a post-COVID-19 environment. *Journal of Community Safety and Well-Being*, *5*, 31–36. https://doi.org/10.35502/jcswb.133

Felson, M., Jiang, S., & Xu, Y. (2020). Routine activity effects of the Covid-19 pandemic on burglary in Detroit, March, 2020. *Crime Science*, *9*(1), 10. https://doi.org/10.1186/s40163-020-00120-x

Grimalda, G., Buchan, N. R., Ozturk, O. D., Pinate, A. C., Urso, G., & Brewer, M. B. (2021). Exposure to COVID-19 is associated with increased altruism, particularly at the local level. *Scientific Reports*, *11*(1). https://doi.org/10.1038/s41598-021-97234-2

Gryszczyńska, A. (2021). The impact of the COVID-19 pandemic on cybercrime. *Bulletin of the Polish Academy of Sciences. Technical Sciences*, *69* (nr 4). https://doi.org/10.24425/bpasts.2021.137933

Hodgkinson, T., & Andresen, M. A. (2020). Show me a man or a woman alone and I'll show you a saint: Changes in the frequency of criminal incidents during the COVID-19 pandemic. *Journal of Criminal Justice*, *69*, 101706. https://doi.org/10.1016/j.jcrimjus.2020.101706

Hu, X., Dong, B., & Lovrich, N. (2022). We are all in this together: Police use of social media during the COVID-19 pandemic. *Policing: An International Journal*, *45*, 106–123. https://doi.org/10.1108/PIJPSM-05-2021-0072

Jarczewski, W. (2022). Praca Policji w okresie pandemii COVID-19 roku 2020. Analiza zadań, poziomu represji oraz zmian tendencji zagrożeń w wybranych kategoriach przestępstw kryminalnych. In M. Tomaszyk & D. Dymek (Eds.), *Środowisko bezpieczeństwa w zagrożeniach epidemiologicznych. Doświadczenia COVID-19 w Wielkopolsce* (pp. pp. 237–259). Wydawnictwo Naukowe Wydziału Nauk Politycznych i Dziennikarstwa UAM. https://doi.org/10.14746/wnpid.2022.9788366740631.14

Komenda Stołeczna Policji. (2020). *Ważny KOMUNIKAT! – powiadamiając o. . . .* Retrieved November 10, 2023, from www.facebook.com/komendastolecznapolicji/posts/2957398060979263

Lum, C., Maupin, C., & Stoltz, M. (2020). *The impact of COVID-19 on law enforcement agencies (wave 1). A joint report of the international association of chiefs of police and the center for evidence-based crime policy.* George Mason University.

Maskály, J., Ivković, S. K., & Neyroud, P. (2021). Policing the COVID-19 pandemic: Exploratory study of the types of organizational changes and police activities across the globe. *International Criminal Justice Review*, *31*, 266–285. https://doi.org/10.1177/10575677211012807

Mehdizadeh, S., & Kamkar, K. (2020). COVID-19 and the impact on police services. *Journal of Community Safety and Well-Being*, *5*, 42–44. https://doi.org/10.35502/jcswb.139

Miller, M. (2020, April 16). FBI sees spike in cyber crime reports during coronavirus pandemic. *The Hill*. Retrieved November 10, 2023, from https://thehill.com/policy/cybersecurity/493198-fbi-sees-spike-in-cyber-crime-reports-during-coronavirus-pandemic/

Ministerstwo Zdrowia. (2020). *Pierwszy przypadek koronawirusa w Polsce – Ministerstwo Zdrowia – Portal Gov.pl*. Retrieved November 10, 2023, from www.gov.pl/web/zdrowie/pierwszy-przypadek-koronawirusa-w-polsce

Mohler, G., Bertozzi, A. L., Carter, J., Short, M. B., Sledge, D., Tita, G. E., Uchida, C. D., & Brantingham, P. J. (2020). Impact of social distancing during COVID-19 pandemic on crime in Los Angeles and Indianapolis.

Journal of Criminal Justice, *68*, 101692. https://doi.org/10.1016/j.jcrimjus.2020.101692

Newiss, G., Charman, S., Ilett, C., Bennett, S., Ghaemmaghami, A., Smith, P., & Inkpen, R. (2022). Taking the strain? Police well-being in the COVID-19 era. *The Police Journal*, *95*, 88–108. https://doi.org/10.1177/0032258X211044702

Nielson, K. R., Zhang, Y., & Ingram, J. R. (2022). The impact of COVID-19 on police officer activities. *Journal of Criminal Justice*, *82*, 101943. https://doi.org/10.1016/j.jcrimjus.2022.101943

Nivette, A. E., Zahnow, R., Aguilar, R., Ahven, A., Amram, S., Ariel, B., Burbano, M. J. A., Astolfi, R., Baier, D., Bark, H. M., Beijers, J. E., Breetzke, G., Concha-Eastman, I. A., Curtis-Ham, S., Davenport, R., Díaz, C., Fleitas, D., Gerell, M., Jang, K.-H., . . . Eisner, M. P. (2021). A global analysis of the impact of COVID-19 stay-at-home restrictions on crime. *Nature Human Behaviour*, *5*(7), 868–877. https://doi.org/10.1038/s41562-021-01139-z

Ostaszewski, P., Klimczak, J., & Włodarczyk-Madejska, J. (2021). *Przestępczość i wymiar sprawiedliwości w pierwszym roku pandemii COVID-19/Paweł Ostaszewski, Joanna Klimczak, Justyna Włodarczyk-Madejska., Prawo Karne*. Wydawnictwo Instytutu Wymiaru Sprawiedliwości.

Portal Gov.pl. (2021). *Koronawirus: informacje i zalecenia. Od 20 marca w całej Polsce obowiązują rozszerzone zasady bezpieczeństwa*. Retrieved November 10, 2023, from www.gov.pl/web/koronawirus/od-20-marca-w-calej-polsce-obowiazuja-rozszerzone-zasady-bezpieczenstwa

Portal Gov.pl. (2022). *Raport zakażeń koronawirusem (SARS-CoV-2) – Koronawirus: informacje i zalecenia*. Retrieved November 10, 2023, from www.gov.pl/web/koronawirus/wykaz-zarazen-koronawirusem-sars-cov-2

Ralph, L., Jones, M., Rowe, M., & Millie, A. (2022). Maintaining police-citizen relations on social media during the COVID-19 pandemic. *Policing and Society*, *32*, 764–777. https://doi.org/10.1080/10439463.2022.2091565

Ribeiro, S., Burkhardt, C., & Caneppele, S. (2021). *COVID-19, crime and criminal justice: Mapping criminological research projects around the world. Research briefs*. Université de Lausanne. Retrieved November 10, 2023, from https://serval.unil.ch/notice/serval:BIB_8D794DDA3C3D

Sampson, R. J., & Groves, W. B. (1989). Community structure and crime: Testing social-disorganization theory. *American Journal of Sociology*, *94*(4), 774–802. https://doi.org/10.1086/229068

Starzewski, Ł. (2020). *Protesty społeczne w dniu wyroku TK ws. aborcji. Policja podsumowała swe działania*. Retrieved November 10, 2023, from http://bip.brpo.gov.pl/pl/content/rpo-protesty-w-dniu-wyroku-ws-aborcji-podsumowanie-ksp

Stogner, J., Miller, B. L., & McLean, K. (2020). Police stress, mental health, and resiliency during the COVID-19 pandemic. *American Journal of Criminal Justice*, *45*, 718–730. https://doi.org/10.1007/s12103-020-09548-y

Volkmer, I. (2021). *Social media and COVID-19: A global study of digital crisis interaction among Gen Z and millennials*. https://minerva-access.unimelb.edu.au/items/db07228d-5b4c-59df-bf3e-e6bb37072aa9

Waszkiewicz, P. Tomaszewska-Michalak, M., Rabczuk, S., & Stromczyński, B. (2021). Czy Wielkopolska Policja umie w internety? Analiza strategii komunikacyjnej KWP w Poznaniu na portalu Facebook. In *Media społecznościowe w pracy organów ścigania* (pp. 61–81). https://doi.org/10.5281/zenodo.4624983

Waszkiewicz, P., Tomaszewska-Michalak, M., Rabczuk, S., & Stromczyński, B. (2023). *Law enforcement and marketing crossroads? Social media publication strategies of polish police*, unpublished.

WHO (2023). *Coronavirus (COVID-19) dashboard*. Retrieved November 10, 2023, from https://covid19.who.int

Wielkopolska Policja. (2020a). *Jeden z mężczyzn, który przebywa na . . . .* Retrieved November 10, 2023, from www.facebook.com/PolicjaWlkp/posts/1542480232575302

Wielkopolska Policja. (2020b). *Jutro przywracamy do pełnej funkcjonalności . . . .* Retrieved November 10, 2023, from www.facebook.com/PolicjaWlkp/posts/1552522708237721

Wirus z Chin. (2020). *Nowe środki bezpieczeństwa na Lotnisku Chopina*. Retrieved November 10, 2023, from www.rynek-lotniczy.pl/wiadomosci/wirus-z-chin-nowe-srodki-bezpieczenstwa-na-lotnisku-chopina-7718.html

Zahran, S., Shelley, T. O. C., Peek, L., & Brody, S. D. (2009). Natural disasters and social order: Modeling crime outcomes in Florida. *International Journal of Mass Emergencies & Disasters*, *27*(1), 26–52. https://doi.org/10.1177/028072700902700102

Związek Przedsiębiorców i Pracodawców. (2021). *Podsumowanie lockdown-u w Polsce*. Retrieved November 10, 2023, from https://zpp.net.pl/wp-content/uploads/2021/01/25.01.2021-Business-Paper-Podsumowanie-lockdownu-w-Polsce.pdf

5 Social media evidence in criminal proceedings

Paweł Waszkiewicz and Krzysztof Worek

Introduction

Social media now serves a multifaceted purpose beyond mere entertainment and communication. Its increasing impact on societies globally is evident in its utilization by law enforcement and criminal justice agencies. Social media evidence is becoming increasingly prevalent, as demonstrated by its use in high-profile cases such as the January 6, 2021, attack on the United States Capitol. Several rioters were identified, prosecuted, and sentenced based on evidence obtained from prominent social media platforms (The Guardian, 2021). At the time of writing, social media evidence is also being utilized on a large scale in the "Freedom Convoy" trial in Ottawa (Canadian Press, 2023). However, social media evidence extends beyond trials related to riots or large public events. In Georgia, USA, in a RICO indictment, prosecutors utilized rap artist Young Thug's public posts and song lyrics as evidence to demonstrate his significant involvement in a criminal organization (Green & Helfand, 2023). In the UK, social media played a pivotal role in the trial of Eleanor Williams, who disseminated fabricated accusations of being raped and trafficked by an Asian grooming gang through multiple real and fake social media accounts (Pidd, 2023). Social media evidence is also becoming increasingly influential in civil trials, as seen in the Michael Blume free speech case in Germany. In its ruling, the Frankfurt court distinguished between opinions regarding the defendant's anti-Semitism and false allegations of pedophilia spread on Twitter (Hessenschau, 2022).

The number of court cases that present social media evidence is increasing in almost every state, and some of these cases are a direct result of lawmakers' calls for the establishment of unique regulations for social media evidence (BBC, 2023). For example, common sense predicts that social media evidence has or will become ubiquitous in divorce cases. In 2019, family lawyers in Warsaw coined the phrase "there is no divorce without Facebook evidence," highlighting the growing prevalence of online activity in legal proceedings (Waszkiewicz et al., 2020). However, this statement's worth is, at best,

DOI: 10.4324/9781032680194-5
This chapter has been made available under a CC-BY-NC 4.0 license.

anecdotal. Empirical investigations on the application of social media in criminal legal procedures will provide insight into this matter.

State of the art

The present ubiquity of social media as an everyday tool in policing may overshadow its relatively short history in the law enforcement toolbox. West Midlands Police likely made the first official use of social media in December 2008 by publishing their inaugural tweet (Crump, 2011), two years after Twitter's inception. Less than three years later, in September 2011, about 88% of law enforcement agencies in the United States had implemented some form of social media public relations strategy (Kim, Oglesby-Neal & Mohr, 2017).

The use of social media by law enforcement as a tool for establishing community policing has been described and analyzed in various works. It has been suggested that social media can facilitate communication and trust-building between police officers and members of the community (Brainard & Derrick-Mills, 2011). However, most publications are "generally theoretical and speculative, accentuating its potentialities, both good and bad, or drawing on exemplary and idiosyncratic cases" (Walsh & O'Connor, 2019, p. 8).

Social media's impact on policing has been the subject of empirical research since the late 2000s. The majority of studies have relied on case studies, for example the UK police's use of Twitter during the riots of 2011 (Denef et al., 2013; Procter et al., 2013) and, across the Atlantic, large-scale public disorder such as the 2011 Vancouver Stanley Cup riot (Trottier, 2012; Schneider & Trottier, 2012). Additionally, several Canadian cities have been examined via case studies (Schneider, 2016). A different methodological approach is to study the social media publishing strategies of law enforcement agencies. The different types of published content have been categorized and examined using various frameworks (Lieberman et al., 2013; Hu et al., 2018).

Only sporadically have law enforcement officers' experiences and opinions been investigated, as in the European COMPOSITE project, where approximately 400 police officers from 22 countries responded to an online survey about the utilization of social media in the workplace (Denef et al., 2012). According to the literature review, by 2021, seven projects had been conducted to collect the personal experiences of police officers (Kargul & Jędrzejak, 2021). Two studies took place in the United States (2012 and 2014), two in Canada (2011 and 2016–17), a multi-country study of 22 European countries in 2012 (COMPOSITE), one in Germany in 2014, and another in India in 2018. An updated review in 2023 discovered four newly published studies since 2021 – two from Poland (2020 and 2021), one from Scandinavia (2021), and one from Canada (2023) (Waszkiewicz, 2024).

The least surveyed aspect of social media in criminal justice practice is the use of social media evidence at trial. Most works on this topic have described and discussed the legal regulations for utilizing such evidence (Browning, 2010; Uncel, 2011; Murphy & Fontecilla, 2013; Powell & Haynes, 2020), analyzing critical issues such as the credibility, integrity, and validity of evidence presented by parties. Without support by empirical evidence, these analyses remain interesting theoretical deliberations. Without support by empirical evidence – anecdotal evidence is not enough – these analyses remain interesting theoretical deliberations.

For this work, an extensive literature review was undertaken, with a particular focus on studies of the use of social media evidence in trials. The review uncovered ten relevant studies: seven conducted in Poland, one in the United States, one in Australia, and one examining six European countries (Bulgaria, Greece, Italy, Latvia, Slovakia, and Slovenia). These investigated a diverse array of legal fields, including civil, family, constitutional, and criminal law. However, the methodology utilized to examine the jurisprudence of the European courts was absent; this includes sampling criteria, variables, and analysis of cases. Thus, the findings are limited to theoretical perspectives supported by the selected cases (Psychogiopoulou, 2021). The Australian study, which analyzed 136 first-instance judgments between 2009 and 2014 from various family courts, including the Federal Magistrates Court (Family), the Federal Circuit Court (Family), the Family Court of Australia, and the Family Court of Western Australia, offers insight into the use of social media evidence in family law. The analysis aimed to determine how and when social media evidence is adduced (Blakeley et al., 2015). Most of the identified judgments (79%) concerned parenting issues, and almost all the evidence came exclusively from Facebook. The study found that social media evidence is rarely rejected (this only happened in 18% of cases), and text is more likely to be viewed as strong evidence (88% of cases) than pictures or video (65%). It also found contradictory judicial decisions in similar cases regarding the acceptance and interpretation of social media evidence (Blakeley et al., 2015).

Similar methodological approaches were employed in a Polish study (Skraba & Strzałkowski, 2021) and the sole identified US study (Graves et al., 2020). The authors utilized legal databases and various keywords to identify cases in which evidence from social media was utilized. Graves, Glisson, and Choo analyzed appellate opinions from the US Ninth Circuit Court of Appeals and the California Court of Appeals from October 2010 to September 2017. Social media evidence was used in 35 federal cases (12 criminal, 23 civil, 0 family) and 923 state cases (552 criminal, 144 civil, 227 family). Among the studied cases, murder was the most frequent charge (317 state cases). Photos or other images were the most commonly used type of social media evidence in federal cases (22%), followed by videos (15%). Posts, statements, and tweets were used less frequently (7% for each). Similarly, in state criminal cases, photos or images were the leading category, followed by videos. In contrast, in state civil cases, posts were the most commonly used type of evidence. In all three samples, social media evidence was primarily used for purposes of incrimination (74% of state and 81% of federal cases). In 14% of cases, both state and federal, social media evidence was used in an exculpatory manner. The studied sample also indicated a significant increase in the use of social media evidence.

Skraba and Strzałkowki's (2021) study analyzed the rulings of all 11 Criminal Courts of Appeal and the Polish Supreme Court between January 2012 and July 2020, identifying 50 cases that involved such evidence. Of the identified cases, 30% were crimes against life and health (primarily murders), and 20% were crimes against sexual freedom. Evidence was sourced from Facebook in half of the cases (n = 26), while one-third did not name the social media platform in question (n = 18). In one-fifth of cases, the evidence was sourced from NaszaKlasa, a Polish school-based social networking service used by alumni and students, which was active between 2006 and 2021. In one-third of cases (n = 18), evidence was obtained from communication between users (messages), with almost all instances being based on posts or comments (n = 17). Pictures posted on social media platforms were presented as evidence in eight cases, representing 15% of the total sample, while the addition of "friends" occurred in two cases. The data showed a minor upsurge in the application of social media evidence.

Six empirical studies concentrating on criminal court proceedings were conducted in Poland between 2020 and 2021 (Chabiera & Klotz, 2022; Chmiel & Korkus, 2022; Chruścińska & Nawara, 2022; Dąbrowski & Nadolny, 2022; Domańska & Czerwiński, 2022; Goliasz & Worek, 2022). These tested multiple hypotheses regarding the use of social media evidence, utilizing a set of variables coded on the full court files in print, instead of relying on legal bases that exclude several rulings and present only selective data. However, the publications were only in Polish, significantly limiting the readership. In this chapter, we gather the results of these studies to analyze and present them as a cohesive whole, to provide an encompassing view of the role social media evidence plays in criminal trials.

Study

The study was part of the "Social Media in Law Enforcement Agencies' Practice" project, and the authors of this chapter participated in its preparation and implementation as principal investigator and researcher, respectively. A group of 11 people also participated in the work: Anna Chabiera, Ewa Chmiel, Katarzyna Chruścińska, Szymon Czerwiński, Filip Dąbrowski, Barbara Domańska, Adam Goliasz, Miłosz Klotz, Martyna Korkus, Jakub Nadolny, and Agnieszka Nawara.

According to the triangulation principle of research methods, it was planned that the above research project, of which these studies are a part, would use more than one method. In addition to the analysis of existing research and legal regulations, a variety of empirical methods were chosen, including interviews and analysis of court files. One of the project's goals, pursued through the described studies, was to analyze the actual utilization of evidence from social media in criminal proceedings. This was achieved by examining already generated court files.

During the subject planning stage of the research, the following research questions were formulated: the first was fundamental, and the others were supplementary:

RQ1: What is the actual utilization of evidence from social media in criminal proceedings?
RQ2: What is the demographic profile of defendants and victims in cases involving evidence from social media?
RQ3: What are the existing methods of handling evidence from social media?
RQ4: What is the characteristic behavior of perpetrators in proceedings where evidence from social media is present?
RQ5: What is the significance of the presence of evidence from social media for the course and outcome of legal proceedings?

To address the research questions, we developed the following hypotheses:

H1: Social media evidence will be found in the investigated case categories.
H2: Cases with social media evidence will differ in the average age of the defendant and the victim compared to cases without such evidence.
H3: Women will more often be victims, and men defendants, irrespective of the presence of social media evidence in a given case.
H4: Evidence sourced from social media will be introduced more often during the preliminary proceedings than during the trial.
H5: Victims will be more likely than defendants to present social media evidence.
H6: Facebook is expected to be the leading service for sourcing evidence.
H7: Publicly posted content is expected to make up most of the evidence presented.
H8: Posts will be the main type of secured content.
H9: The accused will generally have used their first and last names.
H10: The prevalent method of content preservation will be to take a screenshot.
H11: The presented evidence will typically remain uncontested.
H12: The presence of social media evidence will likely result in shorter proceedings.
H13: In cases where social media evidence is present, there will be a higher rate of convictions than in cases lacking such evidence.

Method

Research method

The selected research methodology employed quantitative analysis of court files to achieve the research goal of comprehending the actual utilization of social media evidence in court proceedings. Court files exhibit objectivity (Halicka et al., 2015), as they are data that have not been generated by the research team but produced independently within a rigid procedural system. Unlike survey research, the shape of the obtained responses is not influenced by the subjects being studied (Crofts, 2003). To minimize the influence of the research team members, the analysis of court files utilized a standardized questionnaire comprising mainly closed-ended questions.

Qualitative research was not selected due to the exploratory nature of the study and the objective of covering a large sample of cases. Conducting an in-depth content analysis of the files would not have been feasible; the aim was to gather the widest possible range of information, which would also support future attempts at qualitative research. The chosen methodology and design of the research instrument facilitated conducting the study with minimal susceptibility to distortions caused by human factors, thus yielding highly objective outcomes.

Variables, their operationalization, and the research tool

The variables were selected based on accepted hypotheses. Each court file in the constructed questionnaire was assigned to the corresponding court where the case originated. Legal categorization was determined solely from the court's decision. The gender and age of the accused and victims at the time of the offense were added from the data in the file. The duration of the preparatory and judicial proceedings and their total duration were calculated based on the dates of issuing specific documents or the occurrence of initiating or concluding events for each stage of the proceedings. A list of typical options, as provided by Polish criminal procedure, was created for decision-making. The existence of social media evidence was ascertained by selecting "YES/NO" options. If social media evidence existed, we determined the stage at which it was presented, noting if it was during preparatory or judicial proceedings, and who initiated it. We also recorded the name of the platform from which the evidence came and whether it was public, private, or restricted to a specific group based on its nature. Subsequent inquiries required choosing from a list the manner of securing content, the signature method of its author, and the content securing method. It was also imperative to denote if the evidence was contested and, if so, how. Likewise, it was important to specify if the evidence was incorporated into the verdict – that is, whether the court referred to it during the sentencing process.

The standardized questionnaire comprised a total of 40 items clustered into 15 sections. It was computer-generated, but manual coding of cases was also an option, followed by the transfer of data to the database. For most variables, it offered dropdown lists of suggested responses while also allowing for the provision of answers with different content. The goal of this method was to streamline the response selection process while still being able to incorporate unexpected scenarios without skewing the results.

Course of research

Fourteen local courts (*sąd rejonowy*, *SR*) within the Warsaw Appellate Court District were selected for the study, seven of which are situated within Warsaw city limits and seven in the neighboring counties.[1] These areas exhibit significant demographic diversity; they include the country's largest city, surrounding towns, and rural regions. It must be stressed that this selection of courts does not represent the entire Polish population.[2] However, due to the exploratory nature of the research and lack of claims for generalizing the findings, this sample was sufficient. The study examined cases that were concluded between 2017 and 2019 in the local courts, designated as the first-instance courts. The short time frame facilitated a thorough evaluation of the entire case population, thus reducing the likelihood of random outcomes.

The study comprised multiple stages. First, we gathered data on the size of the population under study. In early 2020, requests were sent to the presidents of all 14 local courts to furnish a list of case numbers meeting the specified time criteria in the study. These requests included data related to a wider range of legal qualifications. Before analyzing the results, we anonymized the courts by assigning a letter from A to N to each. If the identified population exceeded the capacity of the research team, we considered a representative sample of cases with a specific qualification.

Challenges and limitations arose in the process of collecting data from several courts, as evidenced by the responses from Courts G, N, and L. Court G demanded significant effort to obtain the requested data, requiring a demonstration of specific public interest, while Court N offered a timeline for data submission that ultimately produced no tangible results despite multiple attempts at contact. Similarly, Court L provided only partial data, citing the need to reallocate staff and the lack of necessary software. Consequently, Court L did not qualify for further consideration. However, positive responses were received

1 SR dla Warszawy-Mokotowa, SR dla m. st. Warszawy, SR dla Warszawy-Śródmieścia, SR dla Warszawy-Woli, SR dla Warszawy-Żoliborza, SR w Grodzisku Mazowieckim, SR w Piasecznie, SR w Pruszkowie oraz podległe SO Warszawa-Praga: SR dla Warszawy Pragi-Południe, SR dla Warszawy Pragi-Północ, SR w Legionowie, SR w Nowym Dworze Mazowieckim, SR w Otwocku, SR w Wołominie.

2 In Poland, there are a total of 11 appellate courts, 46 district courts, and 319 local courts. They cover areas that vary in terms of size, urbanization, and population density.

from the majority of courts, with the exception of Court K, which cited operational limitations due to the COVID-19 pandemic and was therefore excluded from the study. As a result, the final sample for the study included cases from 10 of the 14 local courts contacted.

Research sample

During the records request phase, the research team analyzed cases from 11 different courts. At that time, it was unknown that Court K would not grant access. The total population of cases was 1,514, consisting of 368 cases of stalking and identity theft, 64 cases of pornography, 893 cases of defamation, 52 cases of hate crimes, 66 cases of animal cruelty, and 71 cases of copyright infringement. Due to the large number of defamation cases, a random sample of 269 was chosen at a confidence level of 95%. However, the rejection by one of the courts reduced this number to 222. Therefore, the total number of cases considered for the study was 843; the review denial by Court K brought this down to 775.

However, it was impossible to review the entire pool of cases due to the outbreak of the COVID-19 pandemic. Many court reading rooms had to operate in a limited capacity during the ongoing research, which significantly prolonged the research timeline and posed a challenge to case analysis. In addition, some cases became inaccessible for reasons such as the transfer of case records to other courts or retrieval by a judge. After considering the relevant factors, the study analyzed a total of 493 cases, including 222 cases of stalking and identity theft, 34 cases of pornography, 116 cases of defamation, 36 cases of hate crimes, 39 cases of animal cruelty, 45 cases of copyright infringement, and 1 involving both stalking and animal cruelty.

During the data processing stage, we excluded cases where judgments were based on varying legal qualifications, incomplete case files, or unresolved proceedings; 478 cases from 10 local courts were then selected for further analysis (Tables 5.1 and 5.2).

Table 5.1 Number of analyzed cases per legal qualification

*Legal qualification**	*Number of cases*	*% of cases*
Stalking and identity theft	211	44.1
Pornography	33	6.9
Defamation	114	23.8
Hate crimes	36	7.5
Copyright infringement	44	9.2
Animal cruelty	39	8.2
Stalking and animal cruelty	1	0.2
Total	478	100

* Within this chapter, all results will be rounded to one decimal place.

Table 5.2 Number of cases analyzed per court

Court	*Number of cases*	*Court*	*Number of cases*
A	90 (18.8%)	F	55 (11.5%)
B	45 (9.4%)	H	51 (10.7%)
C	55 (11.5%)	I	12 (2.5%)
D	44 (9.2%)	J	38 (7.9%)
E	57 (11.9%)	M	31 (6.5%)

Results

The occurrence of evidence from social media

In the examined sample, evidence from social media appeared in 154 cases (32.2%). In 324 cases (67.8%), no such evidence was identified (Figure 5.1).[3]

We found that social media evidence was present in less than 20% of animal cruelty cases, while in three other types of cases (stalking and identity theft, copyright infringement, and defamation), its presence ranged from 20% to 40%. However, in two groups (pornography and hate crimes), the majority of cases contained social media evidence. H1 was, therefore, confirmed.

Age of the accused and victims

To test H2 – that younger individuals use social media more, resulting in lower average ages of victims and offenders in cases linked to such platforms – a relevant comparison was made. Out of the 530 individuals accused in the surveyed cases, 75 were of unknown ages, allowing only 455 to be included in this comparison. Of the 514 victims, the ages of 199 could not be determined due to insufficient data, or because they were legal entities rather than real individuals. Thus, a total of 315 victims were analyzed, as presented in Tables 5.3 and 5.4. The ages of the defendants and victims in cases with social media evidence were compared to cases without such evidence (Figures 5.2 and 5.3). The results were also divided by specific legal qualifications to prevent potential dominance from cases in larger groups.[4]

The findings supported H2: younger individuals were more likely to be accused in cases where evidence from social media was present. Out of the six analyzed categories, five showed a significant age gap between cases with social media evidence and those without. The accused in cases with social

3 In Figure 5.1, one case involving animal cruelty as well as stalking and identity theft has been added to both categories separately.

4 The case involving both stalking and animal cruelty involved one accused, aged 42, and three victims, aged 39, 40, and 41. This case, due to its incidental nature, was not included in the chart.

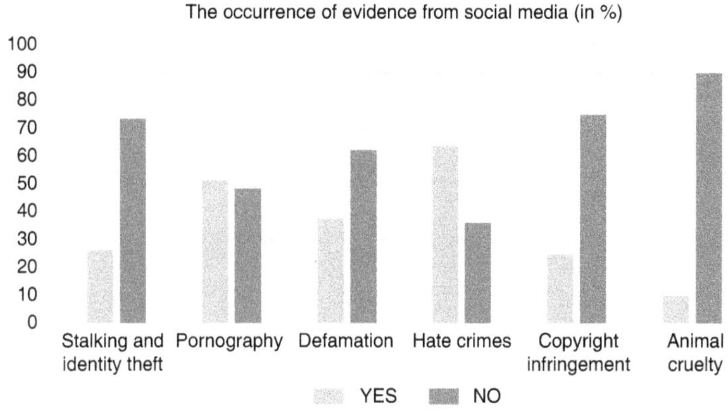

Figure 5.1 Occurrence of social media evidence in each group of cases

Table 5.3 Number of defendants in each category of cases

Legal qualification	*Evidence from SM**	*No evidence from SM*
Stalking and identity theft	58	158
Pornography	22	17
Defamation	30	42
Hate crimes	25	15
Copyright infringement	11	34
Animal cruelty	4	38
Stalking and animal cruelty	0	1
Total	150	305

* SM = Social media

Table 5.4 Number of victims in each category of cases

Legal qualification	*Evidence from SM*	*No evidence from SM*
Stalking and identity theft	56	160
Pornography	5	1
Defamation	19	38
Hate crimes	5	10
Copyright infringement	4	9
Animal cruelty	1	4
Stalking and animal cruelty	0	3
Total	90	225

media evidence had an average age of 36.4 years, whereas in those without such evidence, it was 42.3 years.

In three of the six categories, the average age of victims was lower in cases with social media evidence than in those without. The relationship was reversed

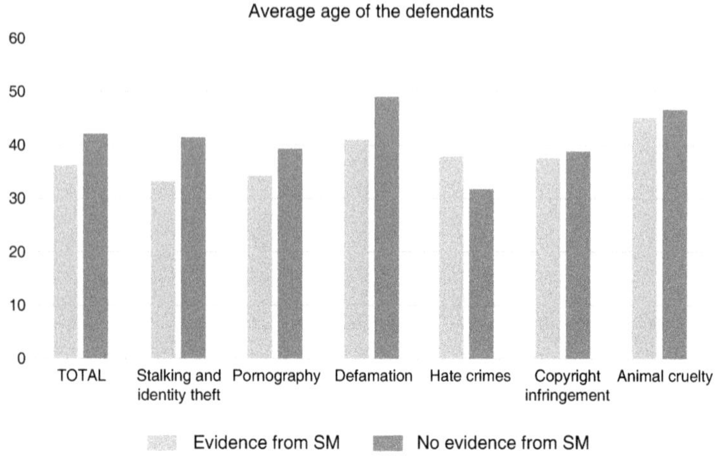

Figure 5.2 Average age of defendants in each category of cases

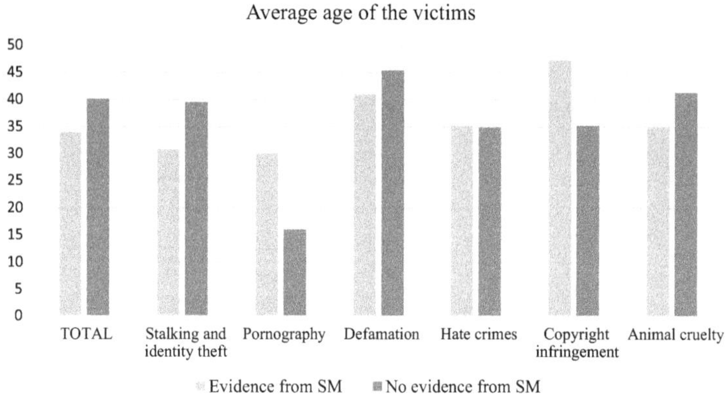

Figure 5.3 Average age of victims in each category of cases

in two groups, while in one group, the average age was almost equal. Notably, the number of known victims was relatively small – only cases related to stalking, identity theft, and defamation had over fifteen known victims. Across the whole sample, victims in cases with social media evidence had an average age of 34, while in cases lacking such evidence, the average age was 40.1. The findings aligned with the hypothesis but were more complex than those observed in the defendant cohort.

Gender of the accused and victims

To test H3 regarding gendered patterns in accusation and victimization, we compared the gender ratios of male and female individuals in both groups. We conducted separate comparisons for cases with evidence sourced from social media and those without. There were 530 accused individuals in all cases, but the gender of 9 was not coded, resulting in a combined sample of 521 accused. A total of 514 victims were identified, but gender information was unavailable for 30 of them, and the question of gender did not apply in 95 cases due to the victim being non-human. Gender analysis was therefore conducted on the remaining 389 victims. Tables 5.5 and 5.6 provide details of the number of accused and victims for each gender, taking into account evidence from social media and the legal qualifications applied.

Some indications supported the hypothesis regarding the defendants. In one of the categories, animal cruelty, the number of female defendants exceeded

Table 5.5 Number of defendants in each category of cases

Legal qualification	*Evidence from SM*		*No evidence from SM*	
	Women	*Men*	*Women*	*Men*
Stalking and identity theft	10	49	35	124
Pornography	0	23	0	17
Defamation	23	25	30	51
Hate crimes	5	20	2	13
Copyright infringement	2	9	9	31
Animal cruelty	3	1	11	27
Stalking and animal cruelty	0	0	0	1
Total	43	119	87	264
	162		351	

Table 5.6 Number of victims in each category of cases

Legal qualification	*Evidence from SM*		*No evidence from SM*	
	Women	*Men*	*Women*	*Men*
Stalking and identity theft	51	7	122	41
Pornography	3	2	1	1
Defamation	14	24	30	44
Hate crimes	3	5	0	11
Copyright infringement	2	2	7	11
Animal cruelty	0	1	4	0
Stalking and animal cruelty	0	0	2	1
Total	73	41	166	109
	114		275	

that of males in cases supported by social media evidence. However, the sample size was small. In all other groups, male-accused individuals predominated. In all cases where social media evidence was available, 26.5% of the accused were women, and 73.5% were men. In cases without such evidence, 24.8% were women and 75.2% were men.

The data collected on victims did not allow a clear confirmation of the hypothesis. Analysis of the entire research sample and subgroups with and without evidence from social media, while disregarding legal qualifications, suggests that women were disproportionately affected. In the group with social media evidence, 64% of the victims were women, and 36% were men; in the group without such evidence, 60.4% of the victims were women and 39.6% were men. However, there were differences at the subgroup level. In cases of defamation and hate crimes, men were more often the victims than women, even when evidence from social media was not present. Similarly, for animal cruelty cases containing evidence from social media, men outnumbered women. In cases of copyright infringements with social media evidence, the results were inconclusive due to the small number of victims in this group.

The stage of the proceedings during which social media evidence was introduced

H4 predicted that social media evidence would be introduced for the first time during the preliminary proceedings. It should be noted that starting from this subsection and continuing through the section on the duration of legal proceedings, we will present and analyze only cases supported by evidence from social media. Since defamation is categorized as a private prosecution offense in Polish law, we did not include cases from this group in our analysis, as the usual preparatory proceedings are not applicable in such cases (see Table 5.7).

Table 5.7 Number of cases in which social media evidence was introduced at each stage with each legal qualification

Legal qualification	*Preparatory*	*Court*	*Both*
Stalking and identity theft	50	3	3
Pornography	16	1	0
Hate crimes	23	0	0
Copyright infringement	9	0	2
Animal cruelty	2	1	1
Total	100	5	6

In line with H4, there was a clear predominance of cases (90.1%) where particular evidence was presented during the preparatory proceedings. Only 4.5% of cases saw the evidence presented during the court proceedings, and in 5.4% it was presented at both stages. This trend was evident in all the reviewed legal classifications.

The initiative to introduce evidence from social media

H5 covered the assertion that victims would be the party that most frequently introduced evidence from social media. In 73.4% of cases, in line with the hypothesis, it was indeed the victim who initiated the introduction of evidence into the proceedings. Occasionally (7.8% of cases), the accused initiated such action. In 2.6% of cases, there was no information available (Table 5.8).

Website of origin for evidence

An analysis was conducted to determine the origins of the evidence from social media in the specific cases. Portals that appeared only once were included in the "Other" category; this comprised a total of 47 websites. However, as some cases had multiple websites from the "Other" category, it was deemed impossible to indicate the percentage of cases; this category was therefore excluded from Table 5.9.

Facebook was the dominant social media platform, present in 51.9% of the cases in which social media evidence was presented. Next was Messenger, which was present in 26.6% of the cases. Instagram appeared in 5.9%; the other social media portals were represented in smaller numbers.

Table 5.8 The number of cases in which social media evidence has been introduced by individual parties to the proceedings, taking into account each legal qualification*

Legal qualification	*Victim*	*Accused*	*Authority*	*Witness*	*No information*
Stalking and identity theft	51	6	2	6	1
Pornography	3	0	14	1	0
Defamation	39	4	0	0	2
Hate crimes	9	1	11	1	0
Copyright infringement	8	1	1	1	0
Animal cruelty	3	0	0	0	1
Total	113	12	28	9	4

* In each case, more than one category could be selected.

Table 5.9 Number of cases involving evidence from specific social media*

Website	*Number*	*%*	*Website*	*Number*	*%*
Facebook	80	51,9	Allegro	3	1,9
Messenger	41	26,6	Skype	3	1,9
Instagram	9	5,8	Gadu-Gadu	3	1,9
Nasza Klasa	6	3,9	Ogłaszamy24	2	1,3
Twitter	5	3,2	Chomikuj.pl	2	1,3
OLX	5	3,2	WhatsApp	2	1,3
Sympatia.pl	4	2,6	No information	3	1,9
YouTube	4	2,6			

* Due to the fact that some of the specified social platforms have a distinctly Polish character, they will be described. NaszaKlasa – a Polish school-based social networking service used by alumni and students, which was active between 2006 and 2021. Sympatia.pl – a dating portal operating since 2003. Allegro – a Polish e-commerce platform operating in six countries in Central and Eastern Europe. It allows interaction among users, including private individuals. Gadu-Gadu – an internet communicator. Ogłaszamy24 – a portal for various types of advertisements. Chomikuj. pl – a website offering file hosting.

Availability of content covered by evidence

Based on H7, it was assumed that evidence content would primarily be public and accessible to interested parties. The results partially supported this assumption; in Table 5.10, these are presented for the entire sample and divided by legal qualifications, wherein the evidence could belong to more than one group.

Although the results confirmed the hypothesis, there were variations between individual legal qualifications. In stalking and identity theft, as well as pornography, evidence from private channels appeared in a greater percentage of cases. In the other categories, public content dominated.

Form of the secured content

Posts were the most frequent type of content used as evidence in proceedings; however, the differences between the individual categories were insufficient for drawing inferences based solely on this. Table 5.11 displays the occurrences of the various forms. Different types of social media data could emerge in each case.

None of the types of social media evidence were present in over half of the cases. The most commonly featured types were posts (39%), messages (38.3%), and comments (29.2%). Profiles/fan pages (18.8%) and photos (14.3%) were also present in more than 1 in 10 cases.

Table 5.14 Questioning social media evidence

Legal qualification	*N*	*Was the evidence questioned?*		
		Yes	*No*	*No information*
Stalking and identity theft	56	5 (8,9%)	49 (87,5%)	2 (3,6%)
Pornography	17	1 (5,9%)	15 (88,2%)	1 (5,9%)
Defamation	43	7 (16,3%)	30 (69,8%)	6 (14%)
Hate crimes	23	3 (13%)	18 (78,3%)	2 (8,7%)
Copyright infringement	11	0	11 (100%)	0
Animal cruelty	4	0	3 (75%)	1 (25%)
Total	154	16 (10,4%)	126 (81,8%)	12 (7,8%)

Duration of proceedings

The duration of the preparatory and court proceedings was analyzed individually, along with the overall duration of both stages. H12 suggested that employing social media evidence would expedite proceedings. However, Figure 5.4 shows that the findings were inconclusive. Only cases with correctly encoded time were considered, comprising the entire pool against which the percentage of cases in each time range was calculated. The coding method involved marking a time range instead of the exact duration of the proceedings; this made it impossible to compute the average duration.

Similar percentages of cases were evident at various time intervals in each of the compared pairs. For pretrial proceedings, the presentation of social media evidence led to a slightly higher percentage of cases being resolved in shorter time frames and a slightly lower percentage in the longest group, although these differences were not significant. The duration of court proceedings was very similar, regardless of the presence of social media evidence. A similar pattern emerged when considering the total duration of both types of proceedings.

Case outcome

The final hypothesis, H13, suggested that social media evidence would result in a higher proportion of guilty verdicts. To test this, the percentages of different case outcomes were compared between cases with and without such evidence. Given the consistent procedural rules for all offenses, specific legal classifications were not differentiated. The results (Table 5.15) indicated the potential validity of the chosen hypothesis. However, as the differences were small, they should be treated with caution.

In both verdict categories used to denote the defendant's guilt – convictions and conditional dismissals – social media evidence was present in a slightly higher percentage of cases. Specifically, 56.5% of cases with social media evidence led to convictions compared to 54.3% without, while 11.7% ended in

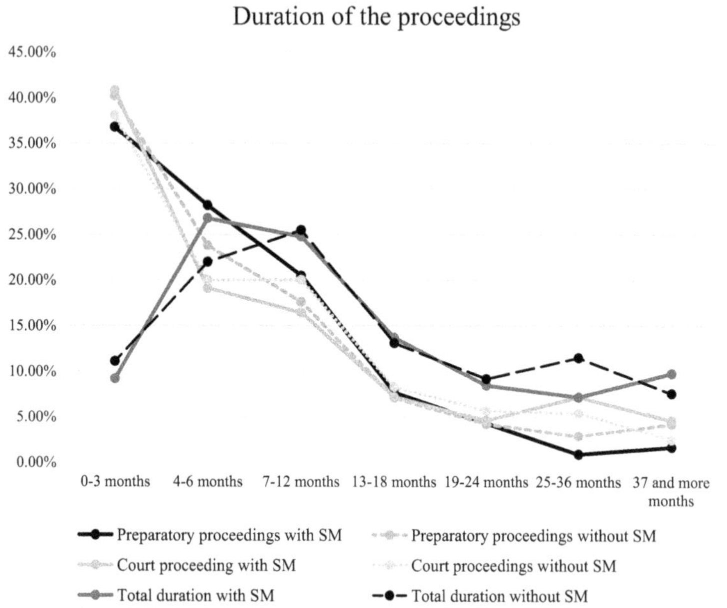

Figure 5.4 Duration of individual case proceedings with and without social media evidence

Table 5.15 Outcomes comparison: social media versus no social media evidence

Outcome	*Evidence from SM (N = 154)*	*No evidence from SM (N = 324)*
Conviction	87 (56.5%)	176 (54.3%)
Acquittal	3 (1.9%)	15 (4.6%)
Conditional dismissal	18 (11.7%)	30 (9.3%)
Dismissal	34 (22.1%)	82 (25.3%)
Other	11 (7.1%)	20 (6.2%)
No information	1 (0.6%)	1 (0.3%)

conditional dismissals compared to 9.3% without. Conversely, slightly lower proportions of cases utilizing social media evidence resulted in acquittals (1.9% compared to 4.6%) or dismissals of proceedings (22.1% compared to 25.3%).

Discussion

Synthesis of the results

This study's findings have several implications. It is noteworthy that social media evidence holds significant popularity in criminal justice practice (H1);

it appeared in nearly a third of cases (32.2%). Cases involving social media evidence often involve younger individuals, as indicated by the lower average age of defendants and victims in this group of cases (H2). This outcome is not surprising given the widespread use of social media across different age groups; although the differences are decreasing, they remain significant. It is worth noting that the average ages of both accused (36.4) and victims (34) were relatively low in this group of cases. They are no longer the youngest adults who have always had social media as a standard part of everyday life; they are individuals who are gradually approaching middle age. These platforms have developed and become popular during their lifetimes.

There were no gender distribution deviations in the groups of accused and victims (H3). Men clearly dominated the former, while women predominated in the latter. This suggests that the type of space (virtual versus physical) probably does not affect crime rates or trends in victimization for both genders, despite the fact that in many situations, the factor of physical strength, usually favoring men, is removed in the virtual realm where contact frequently occurs. The lack of physical interaction did not eliminate gender differences.

This study tested a set of hypotheses that focused on the unique aspects of social media evidence. The research examined the introduction and use of this type of evidence in legal proceedings, as well as the actions of participants following the proceedings. Most of the findings were unsurprising. It was found that evidence is typically introduced during the preparatory phase of legal proceedings (H4). This does not apply to private complaints, such as defamation, which were also analyzed; however, for other legal classifications, the results were clear. In 90.1% of these cases, evidence was presented solely during the preparatory proceedings, and in a further 5.4%, it was presented at both stages. These findings are consistent with the principles of Polish criminal procedure, which require the collection of evidence at this stage of the proceedings.

The study confirmed that this type of evidence is most often provided by victims, who did so in 73.4% of the analyzed cases (H5). The prevalence of victim-generated evidence on social media is a natural outcome, as only a select few have access to private content – typically the accused and the victim. Therefore, the victim has the best chance to employ such material. When content is intended for a specific group or made public, witnesses may also see it, but the victim is the primary individual affected. Complainants typically file a report to obtain the conviction of the individual who committed a specific crime; therefore, it is important for them to present any available evidence.

The results for the frequency of evidence supported hypothesis H6. Facebook had the greatest impact, with Messenger following at roughly half that level, but still at a significant rate. It was necessary to differentiate between these two platforms during document coding despite their shared use. These findings are in line with data on the popularity of particular platforms in Poland and with their primary focus on communication. In contrast to platforms such as Instagram or YouTube, they do not emphasize posting specific content like photos or videos.

Two hypotheses regarding the target audience and format of content can be analyzed together. One (H7) posits that the primary function of social media platforms is to foster community building and social interaction; private content can be shared through alternative channels like email or SMS, but social media offers users the unique capability to publish content publicly, a hallmark of Web 2.0. Posts are the most common type of user-generated content; these can include various forms of material (H8). Furthermore, comments are often used as evidence because they are responses to user-generated content that is at least partially public. Social media has also taken on the roles of various preexisting communication channels, as demonstrated by messages being used as evidence in almost as many cases as posts.

The results for H9 suggest a persistent belief in online anonymity. It is difficult to explain the findings in any other way. Despite numerous awareness campaigns emphasizing that the Internet provides only a false sense of anonymity, 57.8% of offenders used their real identities. It cannot be assumed that the individuals who posted content that later served as evidence were unaware they were committing a crime or were willing to accept potential punishment. Assuming individual rationality, people are generally aware of their actions and do not intend to be convicted.

The findings raise questions about technical expertise in digital content security. Evidence mostly consisting of unverified screen capture printouts was found in 81.2% of cases (H10). Meanwhile, in 81.8% of cases, the accused did not dispute the social media evidence. These results indicate that parties tend to trust online information without thoroughly examining the data. Modifying a screenshot is a simple task that only requires basic computer skills. However, the defendants seem not to have taken advantage of this fact, even though they could potentially have challenged the authenticity of such evidence (H11). Regardless of the veracity of a particular piece of evidence, challenging it could significantly complicate the prosecution's responsibility to demonstrate certain facts. Law enforcement agencies often rely on printouts, even in cases that involve public complaints and preliminary investigations conducted by the agencies themselves. However, authentication of presented materials is not consistently sought; this increases dependence on printouts.

An analysis of the duration of proceedings revealed no significant differences between cases containing social media evidence and those without such material (H12). On the one hand, this type of evidence may not exclude other activities, which could potentially prolong proceedings. On the other, activities related to this type of evidence may increase the time required and negate any potential time savings. Conflicting directives related to adhering to principles of procedural speed and economy, on the one hand, and pursuing the truth, on the other, may contribute to this pattern of evidentiary proceedings.

The concluding hypothesis (H13) suggested that the presence of social media evidence would lead to a higher conviction rate. However, the findings did not definitively confirm this assertion. While the credibility and evidentiary strength of the material may suggest a different outcome, it is important to consider the specificity of the Polish justice system and the notably high percentage of convictions in Poland. Perhaps the high prevalence of convictions leaves little room for cases on the borderline where social media evidence could potentially tip the scales in favor of a conviction. However, social media evidence may have an impact by providing highly visual evidence suggesting the accused's guilt, for example through precisely documented statements.

It has been just over ten years since law enforcement agencies started using social media (Crump, 2011). In a short time, social media has become routine for both law enforcement and society (Kemp, 2023). The significant role of social media in criminal proceedings, as confirmed by this study, is not surprising given its widespread daily use. Social media has been the subject of surveys of law enforcement officers (Denef et al., 2012; Kargul & Jędrzejak, 2021) regarding how they use it in their work. Additionally, researchers have explored the use of social media evidence in criminal proceedings. The increasing popularity of social media has facilitated a shift from theoretical considerations to empirical verification of the issue.

Our study confirms previous findings that Facebook is the dominant platform for gathering evidence, consistent with studies by Blakeley et al. (2015) and Skraba and Strzałkowski (2021). Social media evidence is not often questioned, although the rejection of evidence is generally rare in Polish legal procedure.

Graves et al. (2020) discussed the prevalence of social media evidence in criminal and civil cases. They found that photos and videos were the most common types of evidence in criminal cases, while posts were more prevalent in civil cases. Our study differs from previous findings, as we discovered that criminal cases less frequently involved photos and videos. This is consistent with earlier research conducted in Poland (Skraba & Strzałkowski, 2021). It is important to note that this type of evidence is often used against the accused. It is used for inculpatory purposes (Graves et al., 2020) and is presented by victims to initiate criminal proceedings.

The results depict an intriguing phenomenon: the approach of perpetrators to creating content that later serves as evidence in proceedings. Rational choice theory (Cornish & Clarke, 1987) suggests that criminals will make rational choices associated with the least risk. However, this study found that the actions of defendants during the ongoing proceedings were often difficult to consider rational. The primary behavior observed was the signing of content with personal names (H9). Evidence presented in the form of screenshots (H10) was seldom disputed (H11). Anonymity may still be a significant factor, as it has been since the early days of the Internet (McKenna & Bargh, 2000). The belief that one cannot be identified may motivate perpetrators to engage in certain activities, which may align with the assumptions of rational choice theory based on their knowledge and beliefs. However, these beliefs are misguided.

In the absence or near-absence of safeguards, identifying the content creator should not be particularly difficult (Lewulis, 2023).

Limitations and future research directions

Due to its exploratory nature, this study had limitations. First, the sample selection method and its impact require emphasis. Despite the large sample size, the negative influence of the method for selecting courts undermines the ability to generalize the results to the general population. All courts were from a single appellate court comprised of only two districts. This group of courts may exhibit unique phenomena, potentially connected to their adopted jurisprudential lines. Despite demographic dissimilarities in the court's different jurisdictions, their clustering around one central urban location could produce specific characteristics. It is conceivable that if this study were carried out in regions with differing demographic compositions, such as multiple smaller urban areas, the outcomes might diverge.

Second, the study was limited by its quantitative nature and the construction of the research tool. Quantitative research primarily answers "how" questions while limiting the exploration of "why" questions. This can potentially lead to misinterpretation of the causes of individual results; it also restricts the ability to draw comprehensive conclusions. However, the objectives and nature of this study justify the use of quantitative research as the most appropriate approach. Qualitative research can provide a deeper understanding of the insights uncovered through quantitative research.

Third, this study's methodology for selecting legal classifications for examination may be a limitation. The findings suggest that social media evidence often accompanies these types of crimes. However, it cannot be assumed that all other offenses or criminal activities follow the same pattern of using social media evidence or are equally popular. Other crimes may have a completely different pattern of social media evidence. While the results obtained can be applied to the offenses studied, it is important to exercise caution when extrapolating them to other crimes. This position is supported by the presented findings, which frequently highlight different trends among groups in specific legal classifications.

Conclusions

The verification of H1 alone justifies the need for increased regulation of social media evidence; this is currently inadequate. In Poland, the absence of clear regulations and methodology for handling evidence from social media (Dębniak & Rabczuk, 2019) presents a challenge in developing appropriate procedures that ensure a fair criminal trial. Despite the increasing popularity of social media year after year (Kemp, 2023), legislative actions have not kept up with this trend. Just over ten years have passed since law enforcement began actively using social media; this period is relatively short yet sufficient to implement necessary changes, including legal ones.

However, some perpetrators also may not be keeping up with the technical aspects of social media. Their use of their own names and surnames and their unquestioning acceptance of evidence, even in the form of printouts, without proper justification, may raise significant concerns about their credibility. According to rational choice theory (Cornish & Clarke, 1987), the optimal path is one that offers the greatest possible gains with the least possible risk.

Perhaps none of the opposing parties in criminal proceedings are keeping up with social media. Lawmakers may not be fully prepared to address the use of social media in legal proceedings; perpetrators may not be able to effectively avoid conviction despite available opportunities. It is possible that the findings in this regard are partially misleading, as offenders who use their real names are more likely to be prosecuted than those who use anonymizing techniques. Exploring this would enable more reliable testing of rational choice theory in social media environments.

References

BBC. (2023, March 28). *Eleanor Williams case raised in call for social media rules*. www.bbc.com/news/uk-england-cumbria-65105669

Blakeley, V., Easteal, P. L., Fitch, E., & Kennedy, J. (2015). Social media evidence in family law: What can be used and its probative value. *Family Law Review*, *5*(81), 81–101.

Brainard, L. A., & Derrick-Mills, T. (2011). Electronic commons, community policing, and communication: Online police-citizen discussion groups in Washington, DC. *Administrative Theory & Praxis*, *33*(3), 383–410. https://doi.org/10.2753/ATP1084-1806330304

Browning, J. G. (2010). Digging for the digital dirt: Discovery and use of evidence from social media sites. *SMU Science and Technology Law Review*, *14*(3), 465–496.

Canadian Press. (2023, September 14). In the news today: Social media evidence focus as "freedom convoy" trial continues. *Vernon Matters*. https://vernonmatters.ca/2023/09/14/in-the-news-today-social-media-evidence-focus-as-freedom-convoy-trial-continues/

Chabiera, A. J., & Klotz, M. (2022). Dowody z mediów społecznościowych w sprawach dotyczących przestępstw z nienawiści – praktyka polskich organów ścigania. In P. Waszkiewicz (Ed.), *Media społecznościowe w postępowaniu karnym* (pp. 93–120). Wydawnictwo INP PAN. https://doi.org/10.5281/zenodo.6497160

Chmiel, E., & Korkus, M. (2022). Dowody z mediów społecznościowych w sprawach o zniesławienie. In P. Waszkiewicz (Ed.), *Media społecznościowe w postępowaniu karnym* (pp. 69–92). Wydawnictwo INP PAN. https://doi.org/10.5281/zenodo.6497396

Chruścińska, K., & Nawara, A. (2022). Dowody z mediów społecznościowych w sprawach o czyny zabronione z art. 35 ustawy o ochronie zwierząt.

In P. Waszkiewicz (Ed.), *Media społecznościowe w postępowaniu karnym* (pp. 121–144). Wydawnictwo INP PAN. https://doi.org/10.5281/zenodo.6497377

Cornish, D. B., & Clarke, R. V. (1987). Understanding crime displacement: An application of rational choice theory. *Criminology*, *25*(4), 933–948.

Crofts, P. (2003). Problem gambling and property offences: An analysis of court files. *International Gambling Studies*, *3*(2), 183–197. https://doi.org/10.1080/1356347032000142289

Crump, J. (2011). What are the police doing on Twitter? Social media, the police and the public. *Policy & Internet*, *3*(4), 1–27. https://doi.org/10.2202/1944-2866.1130

Dąbrowski, F., & Nadolny, J. (2022). Dowody z mediów społecznościowych w sprawach o czyny zabronione z art. 202 k.k. In P. Waszkiewicz (Ed.), *Media społecznościowe w postępowaniu karnym* (pp. 45–68). Wydawnictwo INP PAN. https://doi.org/10.5281/zenodo.6497387

Dębniak, H., & Rabczuk, S. (2019). Wybrane aspekty prawne pozyskiwania danych z mediów społecznościowych przez polskie organy ścigania. *Problemy Współczesnej Kryminalistyki*, *23*, 49–78.

Denef, S., Bayerl, P. S., & Kaptein, N. A. (2013). Social media and the police: Tweeting practices of British police forces during the August 2011 riots. In *Proceedings of the SIGCHI conference on human factors in computing systems* (pp. 3471–3480). Association for Computing Machinery, New York, NY, United States.

Denef, S., Kaptein, N., Bayerl, S., & Ramirez, L. (2012). Best practice in police social media adaptation. https://administracionelectronica.gob.es/dam/jcr:e03b0d77-ed32-4f70-9071-cb6a523236ca/COMPOSITE-social-media-best-practice_1_.pdf

Domańska, B., & Czerwiński, S. (2022). Dowody z mediów społecznościowych w sprawach o czyny zabronione z ustawy o prawie autorskim i prawach pokrewnych. In P. Waszkiewicz (Ed.), *Media społecznościowe w postępowaniu karnym* (pp. 145–168). Wydawnictwo INP PAN. https://doi.org/10.5281/zenodo.6497415

Goliasz, A., & Worek, K. (2022). Dowody z mediów społecznościowych w sprawach o stalking i kradzież tożsamości. In P. Waszkiewicz (Ed.), *Media społecznościowe w postępowaniu karnym* (pp. 19–44). Wydawnictwo INP PAN. https://doi.org/10.5281/zenodo.6497404

Graves, L., Glisson, W. B., & Choo, K. K. R. (2020). LinkedLegal: Investigating social media as evidence in courtrooms. *Computer Law & Security Review*, *38*, 105408. https://doi.org/10.1016/j.clsr.2020.105408

Green, W., & Helfand, R. (2023, September 12). Young thug and the YSL RICO trial, explained. *Fader*. www.thefader.com/2023/09/12/young-thug-and-the-ysl-rico-trial-explained-gunna-fani-willis-georgia

The Guardian. (2021, December 13). *Judges weigh social media posts in criminal sentences for US Capitol attack*. www.theguardian.com/us-news/2021/dec/13/judges-weigh-social-media-posts-criminal-sentences-us-capitol-attack

Halicka, M., Halicki, J., Kramkowska, E., & Szafranek, A. (2015). Law enforcement, the judiciary and intimate partner violence against the elderly in court files. *Studia Socjologiczne*, *2*(217), 195–214.

Hessenschau. (2022, November 24). *Bei Pädophilie-Vorwürfen ziehen Frankfurter Richter eine Grenze*. www.hessenschau.de/wirtschaft/verfahren-um-hetze-bei-twitter-bei-paedophilie-vorwuerfen-ziehen-frankfurter-richter-eine-grenze-v4,twitter-vor-gericht-100.html

Hu, X., Rodgers, K., & Lovrich, N. P. (2018). "We are more than crime fighters": Social media images of police departments. *Police Quarterly*, *21*(4), 544–572. https://doi.org/10.1177/1098611118783991

Kargul, P., & Jędrzejak, A. (2021). Wykorzystywanie mediów społecznościowych w pracy organów ścigania – zagadnienia wstępne dotyczące badań zjawiska. In P. Waszkiewicz (Ed.), *Media społecznościowe w pracy organów ścigania* (pp. 19–36). Wydawnictwo INP PAN. https://doi.org/10.5281/zenodo.4624964

Kemp, S. (2023, January 26). Digital 2023: Global overview report. *DataReportal*. https://datareportal.com/reports/digital-2023-global-overview-report

Kim, K., Oglesby-Neal, A., & Mohr, E. (2017). *2016 Law enforcement use of social media survey, report*. International Association of Chiefs of Police and the Urban Institute.

Lewulis, P. (2023). Ustalanie tożsamości polskich użytkowników zagranicznych mediów społecznościowych – studium przypadków ścigania mowy nienawiści w cyberprzestrzeni. *Kwartalnik Krajowej Szkoły Sądownictwa i Prokuratury*, *1*, 73–93. https://doi.org/10.53024/5.1.49.2023

Lieberman, J. D., Koetzle, D., & Sakiyama, M. (2013). Police departments' use of Facebook: Patterns and policy issues. *Police Quarterly*, *16*(4), 438–462. https://doi.org/10.1177/1098611113495049

McKenna, K. Y. A., & Bargh, J. A. (2000). Plan 9 from cyberspace: The implications of the internet for personality and social psychology. *Personality and Social Psychology Review*, *4*(1), 57–75. https://doi.org/10.1207/S15327957PSPR0401_6

Murphy, J. P., & Fontecilla, A. (2013). Social media evidence in government investigations and criminal proceedings: A frontier of new legal issues. *Richmond Journal of Law & Technology*, *19*(3), 11.

Pidd, H. (2023, March 14). Eleanor Williams jailed for eight and a half years after rape and trafficking lies. *The Guardian*. www.theguardian.com/uk-news/2023/mar/14/eleanor-williams-jailed-lying-rapes-trafficking

Powell, A., & Haynes, C. (2020). Social media data in digital forensics investigations. *Digital Forensic Education: An Experiential Learning Approach*, 281–303.

Procter, R., Crump, J., Karstedt, S., Voss, A., & Cantijoch, M. (2013). Reading the riots: What were the police doing on Twitter? *Policing and Society*, *23*(4), 413–436. https://doi.org/10.1080/10439463.2013.780223

Psychogiopoulou, E. (2021). Judicial dialogue in social media cases in Europe: Exploring the role of peers in judicial adjudication. *German Law Journal*, *22*(6), 915–935. https://doi.org/10.1017/glj.2021.57

Schneider, C. J. (2016). *Policing and social media: Social control in an era of new media*. Lexington Books.

Schneider, C. J., & Trottier, D. (2012). The 2011 Vancouver riot and the role of Facebook in crowd-sourced policing. *BC Studies: The British Columbian Quarterly*, (175), 57–72.

Skraba, K., & Strzałkowski, I. (2021). Media społecznościowe jako źródło dowodu w polskim procesie karnym. Badanie orzecznictwa sądów apelacyjnych i Sądu Najwyższego. In P. Waszkiewicz (Ed.), *Media społecznościowe w pracy organów ścigania* (pp. 129–150). Wydawnictwo INP PAN. https://doi.org/10.5281/zenodo.4625046

Trottier, D. (2012). Policing social media. *Canadian Review of Sociology/Revue canadienne de sociologie*, *49*(4), 411–425.

Uncel, M. (2011). Facebook is now friends with the court: Current federal rules and social media evidence. *Jurimetrics*, *52*, 43.

Walsh, J. P., & O'Connor, C. (2019). Social media and policing: A review of recent research. *Sociology Compass*, *13*(1), e12648. https://doi.org/10.1111/soc4.12648

Waszkiewicz, P. (2024). "It's complicated. . . " Social Media and Polish Law Enforcement Agencies' Relationship, *European Journal of Policing Studies*, *7*, doi: 10.5553/EJPS.000016

Waszkiewicz, P., Rabczuk, S., & Worek, K. (2020). Wykorzystanie dowodów z mediów społecznościowych w postępowaniu cywilnym. Perspektywa badawcza. In P. Ostaszewski & K. Buczkowski (Eds.), *Granice prawa. Księga jubileuszowa Profesora Andrzeja Siemaszki* (pp. 763–780). Wydawnictwo Instytutu Wymiaru Sprawiedliwości.

6 Detecting online offenders

A case study of social media hate speech investigations

Piotr Lewulis

Introduction

The emergence of social media in the mid-2000s marked an entirely new period for cybercrime and criminology (Stratton et al., 2017, p. 19). With regard to both forensics and criminology, modern social media create a unique space; they can be seen as digital "crime scenes," platforms for online victimization, and tools for perpetrating socially undesirable acts (Waszkiewicz, 2022, p. 14). Given social media's immense popularity and ubiquity, committing crimes through such platforms is easy. However, effective criminal investigations in such cases can be complicated due to the technical and legal challenges associated with identifying the social media user behind the keyboard and proving their perpetration in a court of law (Arshad et al., 2019; Graves et al., 2020; Jordan, 2020; Silver, 2020). Within this chapter, an "effective" investigation is defined as one that leads to the successful prosecution of the actual perpetrator(s). Investigating and proving social media-related crimes is still an unfinished chapter in legal and forensic research (and likely will remain so due to the ongoing evolution of technical solutions). Qualitative analysis of empirical data, particularly for criminal cases in which the perpetrator was apprehended and tried, can offer a deeper understanding of effective detection and evidence measures; it can also provide criminological insight into who the perpetrators of such crimes are and what their motivations may be.

This chapter briefly discusses what may be understood as "social media crimes" and outlines the most common investigative tactics used by Polish law enforcement authorities to identify online perpetrators. The effectiveness of these tactics is assessed in the context of various online platforms operated by entities both national (i.e., Polish sites offering social media – like functionalities) and foreign (i.e., major international social media platforms). A qualitative case study was conducted to demonstrate how Polish law enforcement and judicial authorities conduct investigations in cases of hate speech on social media. The results of this analysis have been partially published previously in Polish (Lewulis, 2023). Supplementing these findings, this chapter provides added value by focusing additional attention on the perpetrators themselves.

DOI: 10.4324/9781032680194-6
This chapter has been made available under a CC-BY-NC 4.0 license.

Their statements and declared motivations expressed in their depositions are qualitatively analyzed to assess the applicability of the theoretical frameworks used to explain the occurrence of cybercrime. The results support the appropriateness of the strain and self-control theories of crime in the discussed context.

Social media crimes

Despite their ubiquity, social media platforms remain surprisingly difficult to define (Wolf et al., 2018). While there is no single agreed-upon definition, this chapter follows a popular conceptualization by Kaplan and Haenlein (2010, p. 60), who describe them as "Internet-based applications that build on the ideological and technological foundations of Web 2.0, and that allow the creation and exchange of user-generated content." Thus, the term generally refers to a range of platforms that enable users to create content, modify it, share it, and interact with content created by other users (Sloan & Quan-Haase, 2017, p. 17). As their specific functionalities and popularity change and evolve over time (Aichner et al., 2021), this chapter considers any Internet-based platform that follows this concept as "social media," regardless of its prevalence or popularity. Such platforms invite users to engage in self-presentation and self-discourse (Kaplan & Haenlein, 2010, p. 59), allowing them to routinely document their lives and share their thoughts as a new social norm (Kennedy, 2018). Unfortunately, this increases the chances of victimization (Yar, 2012, p. 216).

In legal terms, there is no distinct category of "social media crimes," and the ratio of the number of crimes committed via social media to the total number of cybercrimes is unknown (Dębniak & Rabczuk, 2019, p. 50). Nor has any single definition of "cybercrime" been established; thus, it remains a conventional category despite years of academic debate (Gordon & Ford, 2006; Payne, 2020; Lewulis, 2021b). It is generally accepted that cybercrime has a dual nature: it encompasses both complex, technical crimes and simpler, "traditional" offenses. Ignoring this duality may lead to a misguided notion that cybercrime is always complicated and technical (McGuire & Holt, 2017, p. 77; Miró-Llinares & Johnson, 2018, p. 885; Miró-Llinares & Moneva, 2019). Although certain technology-driven cybercrimes, such as unauthorized account access, malware distribution, or data theft, may indeed be committed in the social media environment, the heterogeneous nature of these platforms and the broad scope of their functionalities can make their use an element of practically any criminal act (Hoffmeister, 2015). Based on individual case studies, social media activities are an essential part of courtroom evidence in a variety of criminal cases, including but not limited to terrorism, murder, domestic violence, fraud, theft, cyberbullying, stalking, and gang activity (Pyrooz et al., 2015; Anwar, 2020; Graves et al., 2020). Online hate crimes are also part of this landscape.

"Hate crime" itself is a broad and elastic concept with multiple meanings depending on the audience and purpose of its use (Chakraborti, 2014, p. 21). One of its manifestations is hate speech. Previous criminological studies have noted its widespread presence in social media cyberspace (Guiora & Park, 2017; Mondal et al., 2017; Müller & Schwarz, 2021). The use of the Internet and social networks easily amplifies hate speech. In this context, "cyberhate" might be an appropriate term; it is defined as "any representation of ideas that promote hatred, discrimination or violence against any individual or group of people, based on aspects such as race, color, ethnic origin, nationality or ethnicity, and religion through digital media" (Castaño-Pulgarín et al., 2021). Hate expressed online can be highly damaging on many levels and has been known to spill over into the real world, augmenting extremist attitudes and offline violence (Castaño-Pulgarín et al., 2021).

Undoubtedly, racism and hate thrive on social media in various forms. Some are associated with user activity, which may be detected and prosecuted, but some forms of discrimination are concealed. Racist dynamics may be embedded in platform governance and design (Matamoros-Fernández & Farkas, 2021) – for example, Snapchat and Instagram's "digital blackface". gif reactions (Jackson, 2017). Out of the many varieties of hate crime, this chapter focuses on instances of hate speech on social media that have led to criminal prosecution and the users who expressed it. Hate speech, as individual behavior, may be subject to criminal liability; of course, the extent of this liability varies depending on the jurisdiction. Importantly, in Poland, certain online statements and comments exceeding the limits of freedom of speech may be subject to public criminal prosecution (Błaszczyk, 2021; Chabiera & Klotz, 2022).

Acknowledging the lack of a coherent, universally accepted definition of "social media crimes," within this chapter, they are defined as criminally prohibited acts committed through social media platforms as the primary space of the perpetrator's activity. The issue will be assessed from two parallel perspectives: first, the investigative capability and detection methods employed by Polish law enforcement and, second, a criminological standpoint, considering the conditions surrounding online hate speech and the perpetrators' underlying motivations for their crimes.

Investigating social media crimes in Poland

The investigative scheme typically followed by Polish law enforcement authorities when trying to establish the identity of any social media crime perpetrator is straightforward. It is based on a two-step process that relies on the cooperation of website administrators and telecommunications companies. First, the police work with website administrators under Articles 217 and 236a of the Polish Code of Criminal Procedure (CCP) to obtain a user's IP address and the precise login time. Second, based on this information, they request the telecommunications company (under Articles 218 and 236a CCP) to provide the data on the subscriber for whom the connection was made. This can only lead to the endpoint device, thereby indirectly identifying a particular person. However, establishing the subscriber of the endpoint device enables further investigative activities – for example, witness interviews may be conducted to identify the person behind the keyboard. This course of action is typical when prosecuting various online cybercrimes (Lebiedowicz, 2022; Taberski, 2018).

The effectiveness of this strategy hinges on factors beyond the control of law enforcement authorities. First, the quality of cooperation with website administrators is crucial. Where the administrators are located outside of national jurisdiction, as is the case with nearly all the popular social media providers, cooperation is usually either hampered, impossible, or time-consuming (Hill, 2015; Nojeim, 2016; Opitek, 2018). Polish national website administrators, however, usually cooperate with law enforcement very efficiently (Opitek & Choroszewska, 2020). Second, even when cooperation with site administrators and telecommunications companies is robust, identifying the user may still pose a challenge if anonymization tools were used.

In certain scenarios, especially given the inefficiency of international cooperation in social media crime investigations, basic open-source intelligence can provide valuable information. Social media users often reveal, either intentionally or unknowingly, personal information (names, surnames, workplaces, schools, lists of "friends" and interests), which may provide the basis for their identification. Good results may come, especially from cross-checking the data from open-source intelligence activities with closed-source intelligence data from law enforcement databases (Day et al., 2016; Karasek, 2018). Such methods are highly cost-effective and may be successful, assuming the suspected user has not taken appropriate measures to maintain their anonymity. Studies to date indicate that many perpetrators, particularly of hate speech, fail to conceal their identity online (Chabiera & Klotz, 2022; Lewulis, 2023). Caution must be exercised as some personal information may not be unique, social media profiles may be fake, or the identity may have been stolen (Karasek, 2018). While accessing openly available user data on the platform, law enforcement officials must also consider applicable privacy laws and ethical constraints on such activity (Williams, 2017; Tomaszewska-Michalak, 2019; Böhm & Lolagar, 2021). There are currently no uniform rules governing this issue across jurisdictions.

Criminological theories applicable to cybercrime

The fact that some social media users have been apprehended and prosecuted might suggest that, from their viewpoint, they were inadequately prepared to commit the crime. They could have employed readily available, advanced means of identity concealment. Previous case studies have already identified two distinct groups of cybercriminals: well-organized "professionals" and "amateurs" (Waszkiewicz, 2022, p. 14). Amateurs, who tend to act spontaneously, are more likely to get caught because they often neglect even the most basic operational security measures. Consequently, such criminals may be relatively easily identified using standard investigative means – either cooperation with social media and Internet service providers or open-source data analysis.

Nevertheless, the reasons and rules behind such spontaneous transgressions are not clear. Despite the pervasive nature of social media in today's world, little is still known about the perpetrators of social media-related crimes or the things that prompt them to act out. Holt and Bossler (2014) noted that only a few studies have sought to apply criminological theories to research on cybercrime. A few years later, Stratton et al. (2017, p. 22) argued that much criminological scholarship is still focused on computing and Internet technologies, either as the targets of crime or as mere tools in the commission of criminologically familiar offenses. Scholars who have attempted to apply criminological theories to cybercrime (including social media crime) have often turned to Routine Activity Theory (RAT) (Cohen & Felson, 1979) to explain the occurrence of most cybercrimes (Marttila et al., 2021; Stratton et al., 2017, p. 21). Originally designed to explain street crime, RAT has been effectively adapted to fit cybercrime (Yar, 2005; Choi, 2008). According to this framework, cybercrimes rely on computer networks to connect motivated offenders with potential victimization targets in the absence of capable guardianship (Reyns, 2017). Undoubtedly, modern cyberspace has no shortage of motivated offenders or potential victims. It also allows for various forms of guardianship, such as site moderation or cybersecurity awareness (Leukfeldt & Yar, 2016).

Although there is a consensus about the general applicability of RAT in explaining many cybercrimes, empirical studies on its applicability to particular types of behaviors have produced somewhat inconsistent outcomes. Leukfeldt and Yar (2016) identified and analyzed 11 self-report studies on the application of RAT (or parts of this theory) to explain victimization in various cybercrimes ranging from malware distribution to stalking and fraud. The results were diverse, showing that some types of criminal activity in cyberspace are better explained within the RAT framework than others. In a follow-up study, Leukfeldt and Yar (2016) tested whether and to what extent RAT helped explain hi-tech crimes (hacking and malware), frauds (identity theft and consumer fraud), and interpersonal offenses (stalking and threats). They concluded that the overall usability of RAT in the discussed contexts has several restrictions, but the theory seems to be especially well equipped to measure malware victimization. Numerous recent studies have demonstrated a statistically significant increase in various types of online crime during the COVID-19 pandemic, a trend attributed to shifts in social habits and increased Internet activity during lockdowns (Hawdon et al., 2020; Buil-Gil et al., 2021; Kemp et al., 2021; Johnson & Nikolovska, 2022). Consequently, the rise in cybercrime in recent years may be credibly explained using RAT.

Nevertheless, other theories of crime, including variations of strain and self-control theories, have also been applied to cybercrime. Their appropriateness depends on the specific type of behavior and its technological context (see Yar & Steinmetz, 2019, pp. 23–48). General strain theory (GST), as proposed by Agnew (1992), appears to provide an appropriate framework for analyzing online hate speech. In short, GST posits that stressful life events causing frustration may lead to transgressive coping responses. This effect may coincide with that described within the self-control theory, which explains crime as a combination of criminal opportunity and the lack of appropriate self-control mechanisms to regulate one's own behavior (Gottfredson & Hirschi, 1990).

Self-control theory has proven helpful in explaining involvement in online behaviors such as posting hurtful information, threatening others through emails or instant messages, and unauthorized accessing of data (Donner et al., 2014). Hawdon et al. (2019) found strong evidence supporting the role of self-control theory, mixed support for social learning theory, and a lack of support for the relevance of RAT in online hate speech perpetration. Strain, low self-control, higher frequency of exposure to offensive content, watching others engage in cyberviolence, and closeness to online communities were all associated with an increased likelihood of engaging in hateful behavior online (Costello et al., 2022; Hawdon et al., 2019). Conversely, low self-control does not predict more technical, better-prepared cybercrimes such as malware distribution (Donner et al., 2014, p. 169; Yar & Steinmetz, 2019, p. 35).

An exhaustive review of the criminological theories applicable to cybercrime is beyond the scope of this chapter. Existing studies suggest these theories show varying degrees of accuracy in explaining different types of online transgressions. One aim of the qualitative case study presented below is to investigate which criminological theories may be best applied to social media hate speech in cases where the investigation turned out to be effective.

Case study methodology

This study aimed to outline some key characteristics of effective social media-related crime investigations. Given its exploratory nature, it did not formulate any preconceived hypotheses. Instead, it addressed general research questions, in line with the assumptions of qualitative research (Creswell, 2009, p. 129). These included: Who are the perpetrators of effectively investigated social media hate speech, and what was their motivation? What investigative means turned out to be effective in identifying them?

The case study analysis was carried out in June 2022; it covered the files of criminal cases concluded between 2016 and 2018 in district courts within the jurisdiction of the Regional Court in Warsaw. Specific cases were manually selected for analysis based on the results of quantitative research conducted in 2019 (Lewulis, 2021a). From the previously examined sample, 11 cases were selected in which the perpetrator had posted various hateful comments on social media. The prosecutor's office classified all these comments as incitement to commit a crime or incitement to hatred based on nationality, ethnicity, or religion – all behaviors that are penalized under Articles 255–257 of the Polish Criminal Code. The research sample for these cases was exhaustive for the indicated period and jurisdiction.

The cases were individually reviewed and analyzed without predefined variables. The examination process entailed in-depth reading of the case files and recording information about the perpetrator's behavior, all the actions taken by law enforcement, and their outcomes. Cases were analyzed from the point of initial information to the final judicial conclusion. The results and findings from the analysis were developed based on detailed research notes prepared during the case file reviews. No personal data was collected. Additional attention was given to the statements made by the suspects in the analyzed cases: Did they admit their guilt? Did they express regret? What justification, if any, did they provide for their actions? The content of these statements was subject to a simple thematic analysis aimed at identifying recurrent themes in the suspect's depositions. This thematic analysis was conducted in Polish using a six-step inductive coding approach, as recommended by Braun and Clarke (2006).

The selected method of qualitative case study analysis has, of course, its distinctive drawbacks (Strumińska-Kutra & Kołdakiewicz, 2012, pp. 1–37). The chosen method uses purposive sampling and does not allow for straightforward generalization of the results or their comparison with results from other studies, particularly those of a quantitative nature. Nonetheless, the case study approach, by definition, allows for the study to be carried out on a relatively small sample chosen in accordance with a particular criterion (i.e., the use of social media for criminal activity) (Flick & Tomanek, 2012, pp. 55–62; Strumińska-Kutra & Kołdakiewicz, 2012, p. 26). The general purpose of qualitative research is to yield an in-depth description rather than a numerical generalization (Bryman, 2016, p. 380). In this context, court case files are particularly suited for qualitative analysis as they document – typically in chronological order – specific legally relevant events and investigative conclusions (Anwar, 2020; Łuczewski & Bednarz-Łuczewska, 2012, p. 163).

The second significant limitation is that only those cases in which the law enforcement authorities successfully concluded the detection process were included in the analysis. These cases offer a picture only of the investigations that were effective and achieved a judicial conclusion. Such cases may be substantively and criminologically different from those in which the perpetrator remained uncaught. This limitation was chosen deliberately to present the key characteristics of effective criminal proceedings. Future research should address this gap by analyzing the investigative challenges in cases where the perpetrators of "social media crimes" avoided criminal liability.

Results and analysis

The analysis included 11 criminal cases with the following case signatures: III K 827/16 (District Court for the Capital City of Warsaw), V K 725/14, IV K 867/16 (District Court for Wola District in Warsaw), XIV K 2/16, VIII K 117/16 (District Court for Mokotów District in Warsaw), II K 231/17, II K 1099/17, II K 1026/16, II K 775/15 (District Court for Śródmieście District in Warsaw), II K 867/17, II K 609/17 (District Court in Piaseczno). For clarity in the description, these cases were numbered (1–11) in the order provided above.

Each case was initiated in response to complaints filed either by offended victims or by a non-governmental organization dedicated to monitoring social media content. All cases shared some common factors: they could all be classified as social media crimes (as defined within this chapter), and the criminal investigations successfully uncovered the identities of the social media users involved, who subsequently had to face the consequences of their actions. All the posts investigated may be considered offensive, xenophobic, racist, and/or advocating violence, and all were classified by the prosecutor's office as incitement to commit a crime or incitement to hatred based on nationality, ethnicity, or religion. To avoid unnecessary exposure, the specific content of these posts will not be quoted in this analysis.

A significant factor that determined the investigative measures used was the "location" of the offense. Of the 11 analyzed cases, 5 concerned user activities on Polish websites with social media functionalities: wiocha.pl, cda.pl, wp.pl, sadistic.pl, and gazeta.pl. The remaining 6 cases concerned user activities on Facebook. During the examined period, no other concluded online hate speech court cases were identified.

In all cases in which the suspects acted in "Polish cyberspace," they were identified based on cooperation with website administrators (who provided IP addresses, connection times, and port numbers to law enforcement officials) and telecommunications companies (who, on that basis, provided the end-subscriber's data). In three cases, to identify the person using the computer, it was also necessary to interview the subscriber and other members of their household. In all six cases concerning Facebook activity, the perpetrators were identified solely based on the data they provided in their profiles. These open-source investigations were extensively recounted in a previous publication in Polish (Lewulis, 2023), but it needs to be briefly repeated that these users' identities were determined by checking the databases available to the police using the users' names, surnames, workplaces, and attended schools, or by interviewing persons listed as "friends" of the suspected user. Determining the identity of users of Polish websites did not pose any difficulties for law enforcement. Identifying Facebook users was more difficult but made easier by the fact that it is relatively common to use real personal data on this particular social media platform.

One of the cases resulted in acquittal, as the court determined that the posted comment fell within the bounds of acceptable criticism. The others were resolved in one of two ways: in five, the accused was found guilty; in the other five, the investigation was conditionally terminated (which also requires an admission of guilt). All the accused accepted responsibility for their comments. In other words, none of the accused disputed that they had posted the contentious comment online. Of the accused individuals, nine (excluding Cases 5 and 9, where the accused chose not to provide a statement, exercising their right to remain silent) offered more or less detailed explanations for their behavior when interviewed by the police or the court. The content of their depositions was subjected to a qualitative analysis to assess their behavior in the context of the possibly applicable criminological theories.

Most suspects, when confronted with their hateful comments, admitted their guilt and expressed regret. This was often conveyed directly in their statement protocol:

- [Case 1] "I admit my guilt and apologize. As soon as I realized what had happened, I removed my comment out of shame."
- [Case 3] "I regret all my comments and I am deeply sorry if I have offended anyone."
- [Case 6] "I deeply regret"; "I have no prejudice against people of other nationalities; my former husband, with whom I have good relations, is from India."
- [Case 7] "I am not racist; I deeply regret posting this comment."

In four cases, however, the perpetrator did not express remorse. The accused in Case 4 argued that the comment was within the limits of permissible criticism; in Case 5, the accused admitted their guilt but refused to offer any explanation; and in Case 9, the accused declined to give a statement and was subsequently acquitted. Case 11 was qualitatively different, as the accused defended their online comments and presented them as political views, stating, "I wrote that comment because I can see what is happening in Europe. I mean . . . they dispersed across Europe and are conspiring against us."

Except for the accused in Case 11, the perpetrators often struggled to specify a precise cause for their actions. They pointed, not always coherently, to various external factors – often a combination of several – that had pushed them to post an aggressive comment. Similar themes seemed to appear in their explanations, such as the consumption of alcohol, agitation from other materials watched online or other comments, emotional tension brought on by personal issues, or humor (i.e., that they thought their post would be funny):

- [Case 1] "I was drunk because I was celebrating my son's birthday"; "I was inspired by a post written by another user"; "I did it under the influence of emotional arousal."

- [Case 2] "There was an article about refugees with many critical comments and, wanting to fit in, I placed my comment, thinking it would be humorous"; "I had had a few drinks and thought of it as a joke"; "I recently lost my job."
- [Case 3] "I commented on a video about the vandalization of a bus in France and posted the comment because I was disgusted that they were breaking the peace there"; "Today, I don't understand why I wrote such posts"; "The only explanation is that I was going through some personal difficulties which caused me to become depressed."
- [Case 6] "I wrote the comment under the influence of emotion after reading the article and watching the video in it."
- [Case 7] "I thought the post was humorous, I have no racist prejudices"; "Writing the comment, I wanted to sarcastically respond to another comment that had been insulting Polish people."
- [Case 8] "When I posted this comment I was under the influence of alcohol"; "I'm tolerant, it was a mistake"; "I was provoked by a video I watched online."
- [Case 10] "I don't know what prompted me to post the comment. I did it after reading other similar posts, and under the influence of emotions."

The contents of the suspects' statements in Cases 1, 2, 3, 6, 7, 8, and 10 were analyzed in order to identify and label the recurring messages, following the methodology of thematic analysis (Braun & Clarke, 2006). After the initial reading, a line-by-line inductive coding was performed; the codes were subsequently grouped to define the dominant themes. The most prominent theme across all these cases was the influence of emotions and external influences, such as alcohol, celebration, and peer pressure. The second and third themes that emerged were mistaken identity and intent (each person appeared to have posted something out of their self-perceived character) and self-reflection (each person expressed regret and/or confusion about why they felt it necessary to post such a comment in the first place).

Discussion and conclusions

Two main conclusions may be drawn from this study: one considering the forensic investigative process in online hate speech cases and one of a more general criminological nature pertaining to the perpetrator's motivations in such cases.

First, from an investigative perspective, two distinct yet non-mutually exclusive detection frameworks seem to be in use by Polish law enforcement authorities in relation to social media hate speech crimes: one based on data provided by third parties (cooperation with website administrators and telecommunications companies), and one based on open-source information from social media user accounts. The first strategy is always effective, but only if the offense took place entirely in "Polish" cyberspace (i.e., on sites administered by entities operating within the national jurisdiction). There are many such entities, and hateful comments often appear on Polish websites. On the other hand, in all the analyzed cases involving foreign social media (in the analyzed cases, Facebook) that have been concluded in court, suspects were identified based on personal information disclosed voluntarily or semi-voluntarily on their profiles.

Second, from a criminological perspective, all the individuals who were effectively prosecuted for social media hate speech in the analyzed cases could be classified as spontaneous amateurs, posting hateful comments while under the influence of strong temporary emotions. These emotions could be triggered by various external stimuli, such as watching an online video or reading an article or other comments, or by internal emotional distress caused, for instance, by job loss or personal difficulties. In some cases, additional factors, like alcohol consumption, may have negatively affected self-control. These characteristics of social media hate crime perpetrators align with strain and self-control theories of crime. As suggested in previous quantitative studies (Donner et al., 2014; Hawdon et al., 2019; Costello et al., 2022), strain and a lack of self-control appear to increase the propensity to engage in hateful activity online. This study adds a qualitative element to these observations, grounded in the actual statements of real perpetrators and the explanations they offered under interrogation in criminal proceedings. Self-control and strain theories seem to be well suited to explaining the occurrence of hate speech on social media. A better understanding of the causes and factors influencing the occurrence of hate speech in cyberspace can contribute to the development of future interventions aimed at its reduction.

However, it must be noted that only cases in which the perpetrators had a basic, uncomplicated modus operandi reached a court of law. The effectiveness of prosecuting social media hate speech seems to have been determined by the choices made by the perpetrators: whether they acted on Polish or foreign social media sites, whether they kept their accounts anonymous, and whether they denied or admitted their guilt when interrogated. In a way, this suggests the powerlessness of law enforcement officials, whose success depends on these simple choices. The behaviors of the perpetrators in the discussed cases are, however, to a certain extent predictable. As such, they are well suited to the application of crime-scripting, a well-established method for creating detailed models describing sequences of predictable actions undertaken by perpetrators in the commission of a crime (Cornish, 1994; Dehghanniri & Borrion, 2021). The preparation of appropriate scripts for social media hate speech, taking into consideration current technological realities, may be a valuable element in future efforts aimed at organizing and harmonizing investigative procedures.

Importantly, the case analysis presented in this chapter included an exhaustive sample of *all* the cases of hate speech crimes on social media submitted to the judicial authorities in the Warsaw metropolitan area within the three-year period under study. The apparent limitation of this study is that it does not account for the unknown number of cases dismissed and discontinued without an indictment being filed due to the impossibility of establishing the perpetrator's identity. It seems that justice reaches those spontaneous amateurs who mask their actions inefficiently.

References

Agnew, R. (1992). Foundation for a general strain theory of crime and delinquency*. *Criminology*, *30*(1), 47–88. https://doi.org/10.1111/j.1745-9125.1992.tb01093.x

Aichner, T., Grünfelder, M., Maurer, O., & Jegeni, D. (2021). Twenty-five years of social media: A review of social media applications and definitions from 1994 to 2019. *Cyberpsychology, Behavior, and Social Networking*, *24*(4), 215–222. https://doi.org/10.1089/cyber.2020.0134

Anwar, T. (2020). Unfolding the past, proving the present: Social media evidence in terrorism finance court cases. *International Political Sociology*, *14*(4), 382–398. https://doi.org/10.1093/ips/olaa006

Arshad, H., Jantan, A., & Omolara, E. (2019). Evidence collection and forensics on social networks: Research challenges and directions. *Digital Investigation*, *28*, 126–138. https://doi.org/10.1016/j.diin.2019.02.001

Błaszczyk, M. (2021). Odpowiedzialność za przestępstwa „mowy nienawiści" stypizowane w art. 256 § 1 i 257 k.k. – Wybrane problemy normatywne i praktyczne. *Studia Iuridica*, *88*, 9–25. https://doi.org/10.31338/2544-3135.si.2021-88.1

Böhm, I., & Lolagar, S. (2021). Open-source intelligence. *International Cybersecurity Law Review*, *2*(2), 317–337. https://doi.org/10.1365/s43439-021-00042-7

Braun, V., & Clarke, V. (2006). Using thematic analysis in psychology. *Qualitative Research in Psychology*, *3*(2), 77–101. https://doi.org/10.1191/1478088706qp063oa

Bryman, A. (2016). *Social research methods* (5th ed.). Oxford University Press.

Buil-Gil, D., Miró-Llinares, F., Moneva, A., Kemp, S., & Díaz-Castaño, N. (2021). Cybercrime and shifts in opportunities during COVID-19: A preliminary analysis in the UK. *European Societies*, *23*(sup1), S47–S59. https://doi.org/10.1080/14616696.2020.1804973

Castaño-Pulgarín, S. A., Suárez-Betancur, N., Vega, L. M. T., & López, H. M. H. (2021). Internet, social media, and online hate speech. Systematic review. *Aggression and Violent Behavior*, *58*, 101608. https://doi.org/10.1016/j.avb.2021.101608

Chabiera, A., & Klotz, M. (2022). Dowody z mediów społecznościowych w sprawach dotyczących przestępstw z nienawiści – Praktyka polskich organów ścigania. In P. Waszkiewicz (Ed.), *Media społecznościowe w postępowaniu karnym*. INP PAN.

Chakraborti, N. (2014). *Framing the boundaries of hate crime*. Routledge Handbooks Online. https://doi.org/10.4324/9780203578988.ch1

Choi, K. (2008). Computer crime victimization and integrated theory: An empirical assessment. *International Journal of Cyber Criminology*. www.semantic

scholar.org/paper/Computer-Crime-Victimization-and-Integrated-Theory%3A-Choi/3c97233b35a7b7b537ff4d3c6db8aeb5e59911f4

Cohen, L. E., & Felson, M. (1979). Social change and crime rate trends: A routine activity approach. *American Sociological Review*, *44*(4), 588. https://doi.org/10.2307/2094589

Cornish, D. (1994). Crimes as scripts. In *Proceedings of the international seminar on environmental criminology and crime analysis* (Vol. 1, pp. 30–45). Florida Criminal Justice Executive Institute.

Costello, M., Reichelmann, A. V., & Hawdon, J. (2022). Utilizing criminological theories to predict involvement in cyberviolence among the iGeneration. *Sociological Spectrum*, *42*(4–6), 260–277. https://doi.org/10.1080/02732173.2022.2105767

Creswell, J. W. (2009). *Research design: Qualitative, quantitative, and mixed methods approaches* (3rd ed.). SAGE.

Day, T., Gibson, H., & Ramwell, S. (2016). Fusion of OSINT and non-OSINT data. In B. Akhgar, P. S. Bayerl, & F. Sampson (Eds.), *Open source intelligence investigation: From strategy to implementation* (pp. 133–152). Springer International Publishing. https://doi.org/10.1007/978-3-319-47671-1_9

Dębniak, H., & Rabczuk, S. (2019). Wybrane aspekty prawne pozyskiwania danych z mediów społecznościowych przez polskie organy ścigania. *Problemy Współczesnej Kryminalistyki*, *XXIII*, 49–78.

Dehghanniri, H., & Borrion, H. (2021). Crime scripting: A systematic review. *European Journal of Criminology*, *18*(4), 504–525. https://doi.org/10.1177/1477370819850943

Donner, C. M., Marcum, C. D., Jennings, W. G., Higgins, G. E., & Banfield, J. (2014). Low self-control and cybercrime: Exploring the utility of the general theory of crime beyond digital piracy. *Computers in Human Behavior*, *34*, 165–172. https://doi.org/10.1016/j.chb.2014.01.040

Flick, U., & Tomanek, P. (2012). *Projektowanie badania jakosciowego*. Wydawnictwo Naukowe PWN.

Gordon, S., & Ford, R. (2006). On the definition and classification of cybercrime. *Journal in Computer Virology*, *2*(1), 13–20. https://doi.org/10.1007/s11416-006-0015-z

Gottfredson, M. R., & Hirschi, T. (1990). *A general theory of crime*. Stanford University Press.

Graves, L., Glisson, W. B., & Choo, K.-K. R. (2020). LinkedLegal: Investigating social media as evidence in courtrooms. *Computer Law & Security Review*, *38*, 105408. https://doi.org/10.1016/j.clsr.2020.105408

Guiora, A., & Park, E. A. (2017). Hate speech on social media. *Philosophia*, *45*(3), 957–971. https://doi.org/10.1007/s11406-017-9858-4

Hawdon, J., Costello, M., Barrett-Fox, R., & Bernatzky, C. (2019). The perpetuation of online hate: A criminological analysis of factors associated with participating in an online attack. *Journal of Hate Studies*, *15*(1), Article 1. https://doi.org/10.33972/jhs.166

Hawdon, J., Parti, K., & Dearden, T. E. (2020). Cybercrime in America amid COVID-19: The initial results from a natural experiment. *American Journal of Criminal Justice*, *45*(4), 546–562. https://doi.org/10.1007/s12103-020-09534-4

Hill, J. (2015, January 28). Problematic alternatives: MLAT reform for the digital age. *Harvard National Security Journal*. https://harvardnsj.org/2015/01/problematic-alternatives-mlat-reform-for-the-digital-age/

Hoffmeister, T. (2015). The challenges of preventing and prosecuting social media crimes. *Pace Law Review*, *35*(1), 115.

Holt, T. J., & Bossler, A. M. (2014). An assessment of the current state of cybercrime scholarship. *Deviant Behavior*, *35*(1), 20–40. https://doi.org/10.1080/01639625.2013.822209

Jackson, L. (2017). We need to talk about digital blackface in reaction GIFs. *TeenVogue*. www.teenvogue.com/story/digital-blackface-reaction-gifs

Johnson, S. D., & Nikolovska, M. (2022). The effect of COVID-19 restrictions on routine activities and online crime. *Journal of Quantitative Criminology*. https://doi.org/10.1007/s10940-022-09564-7

Jordan, C. (2020). *Discovery of social media evidence in legal proceedings*. American Bar Association. www.americanbar.org/groups/gpsolo/publications/gpsolo_ereport/2020/january-2020/discovery-social-media-evidence-legal-proceedings/

Kaplan, A. M., & Haenlein, M. (2010). Users of the world, unite! The challenges and opportunities of social media. *Business Horizons*, *53*(1), 59–68. https://doi.org/10.1016/j.bushor.2009.09.003

Karasek, P. (2018). Social media intelligence as a tool for immigration and national security purposes. *Przegląd Bezpieczeństwa Wewnętrznego*, *10*(19), 405–415.

Kemp, S., Buil-Gil, D., Moneva, A., Miró-Llinares, F., & Díaz-Castaño, N. (2021). Empty streets, busy internet: A time-series analysis of cybercrime and fraud trends during COVID-19. *Journal of Contemporary Criminal Justice*, *37*(4), 480–501. https://doi.org/10.1177/10439862211027986

Kennedy, J. (2018). Oversharing is the norm. In A. S. Dobson, B. Robards, & N. Carah (Eds.), *Digital intimate publics and social media* (pp. 265–280). Springer International Publishing. https://doi.org/10.1007/978-3-319-97607-5_16

Lebiedowicz, A. (2022). Wybrane aspekty prawnokarne, kryminalistyczne i kryminologiczne cyberprzestępczości. *Kwartalnik Krajowej Szkoły Sądownictwa i Prokuratury*, *45*(1), 27–67. https://doi.org/10.53024/2.1.45.2022

Leukfeldt, E. R., & Yar, M. (2016). Applying routine activity theory to cybercrime: A theoretical and empirical analysis. *Deviant Behavior*, *37*(3), 263–280. https://doi.org/10.1080/01639625.2015.1012409

Lewulis, P. (2021a). *Dowody cyfrowe – teoria i praktyka kryminalistyczna w polskim postępowaniu karnym*. University of Warsaw Press. https://doi.org/10.31338/uw.9788323548027

Lewulis, P. (2021b). O rozgraniczeniu definicyjnym pomiędzy przestępczością "cyber" i "komputerową" dla celów praktycznych i badawczych. *Prokuratura i Prawo*, *3*, 12–32.

Lewulis, P. (2023). Ustalanie tożsamości polskich użytkowników zagranicznych mediów społecznościowych – studium przypadków ścigania mowy nienawiści w cyberprzestrzeni [Determining the identity of social media users in Poland: Prosecuting hate speech in cyberspace – a case study]. *Kwartalnik Krajowej Szkoły Sądownictwa i Prokuratury*, 73–93. https://doi.org/10.53024/5.1.49.2023

Łuczewski, M., & Bednarz-Łuczewska, P. (2012). Analiza dokumentów zastanych. In D. Jemielniak (Ed.), *Badania jakościowe – Metody i narzędzia*. Wydawnictwo Naukowe PWN.
Marttila, E., Koivula, A., & Räsänen, P. (2021). Cybercrime victimization and problematic social media use: Findings from a nationally representative panel study. *American Journal of Criminal Justice*, *46*(6), 862–881. https://doi.org/10.1007/s12103-021-09665-2
Matamoros-Fernández, A., & Farkas, J. (2021). Racism, hate speech, and social media: A systematic review and critique. *Television & New Media*, *22*(2), 205–224. https://doi.org/10.1177/1527476420982230
McGuire, M., & Holt, T. J. (Eds.). (2017). *The Routledge handbook of technology, crime and justice*. Routledge/Taylor & Francis Group.
Miró-Llinares, F., & Johnson, S. D. (2018). Cybercrime and place: Applying environmental criminology to crimes in cyberspace. In G. J. N. Bruinsma & S. D. Johnson (Eds.), *The Oxford handbook of environmental criminology* (p. 0). Oxford University Press. https://doi.org/10.1093/oxfordhb/9780190279707.013.39
Miró-Llinares, F., & Moneva, A. (2019). What about cyberspace (and cybercrime alongside it)? A reply to Farrell and Birks "did cybercrime cause the crime drop?" *Crime Science*, *8*(1), 12. https://doi.org/10.1186/s40163-019-0107-y
Mondal, M., Silva, L. A., & Benevenuto, F. (2017). A measurement study of hate speech in social media. In *Proceedings of the 28th ACM conference on hypertext and social media* (pp. 85–94). https://doi.org/10.1145/3078714.3078723
Müller, K., & Schwarz, C. (2021). Fanning the flames of hate: Social media and hate crime. *Journal of the European Economic Association*, *19*(4), 2131–2167. https://doi.org/10.1093/jeea/jvaa045
Nojeim, G. (2016). When other governments want your stuff: Rules of the road for cross-boarder law enforcement demands. *Georgetown Law Technology Review*, *1*, 130.
Opitek, P. (2018). Wybrane aspekty pozyskiwania dowodów cyfrowych w sprawach karnych. *Prokuratura i Prawo*, *7–8*, 65–85.
Opitek, P., & Choroszewska, A. (2020). Uzyskiwanie dowodów cyfrowych z zagranicy w sprawach karnych – Stan obecny i procedowane zmiany (cz. I). *Prokuratura i Prawo*, *9*, 127–149.
Payne, B. K. (2020). Defining cybercrime. In T. J. Holt & A. M. Bossler (Eds.), *The Palgrave handbook of international cybercrime and cyberdeviance* (pp. 3–25). Springer International Publishing. https://doi.org/10.1007/978-3-319-78440-3_1
Pyrooz, D. C., Decker, S. H., & Moule, R. K. (2015). Criminal and routine activities in online settings: Gangs, offenders, and the internet. *Justice Quarterly*, *32*(3), 471–499. https://doi.org/10.1080/07418825.2013.778326
Reyns, B. W. (2017). Routine activity theory and cybercrime: A theoretical appraisal and literature review. In *Technocrime and criminological theory*. Routledge.
Silver, L. A. (2020). The unclear picture of social media evidence. *Manitoba Law Journal*, *43*, 111.
Sloan, L., & Quan-Haase, A. (Eds.). (2017). *The SAGE handbook of social media research methods*. SAGE.
Stratton, G., Powell, A., & Cameron, R. (2017). Crime and justice in digital society: Towards a "digital criminology"? *International Journal for Crime,*

Justice and Social Democracy, *6*(2), 17–33. https://doi.org/10.5204/ijcjsd.v6i2.355

Strumińska-Kutra, M., & Kołdakiewicz, I. (2012). Studium przypadku. In D. Jemielniak (Ed.), *Badania jakościowe – Metody i narzędzia*. Wydawnictwo Naukowe PWN.

Taberski, D. (2018). Postępowania w sprawach o oszustwa popełnione za pośrednictwem Internetu. *Prokuratura i Prawo*, *6*, 63–83.

Tomaszewska-Michalak, M. (2019). Prawne aspekty pozyskiwania informacji w Internecie. *Studia Politologiczne*, *54*, 116–134.

Waszkiewicz, P. (2022). *Media społecznościowe w postępowaniu karnym*. INP PAN.

Williams, J. (2017). Legal and ethical issues surrounding open source research for law enforcement purposes. In A. Skaržauskienė & N. Gudelienė (Eds.), *4th European conference on social media (ECSM 2017): Vilnius, Lithuania, 3–4 July 2017* (pp. 398–404). Curran Associates, Inc.

Wolf, M., Sims, J., & Yang, H. (2018). Social media? What social media? *UK Academy for Information Systems Conference Proceedings*, *3*. https://aisel.aisnet.org/cgi/viewcontent.cgi?article=1002&context=ukais2018

Yar, M. (2005). The novelty of "cybercrime": An assessment in light of routine activity theory. *European Journal of Criminology*, *2*(4), 407–427. https://doi.org/10.1177/147737080556056

Yar, M. (2012). E-crime 2.0: The criminological landscape of new social media. *Information & Communications Technology Law*, *21*(3), 207–219. https://doi.org/10.1080/13600834.2012.744224

Yar, M., & Steinmetz, K. (2019). *Cybercrime and society* (3rd ed.). SAGE.

7 Social media and criminal justice, a complicated relationship

Conclusions

Paweł Waszkiewicz

The aim of the project *Social Media in Law Enforcement Practice* was to analyze the extent and methods of social media use by criminal justice institutions in Poland, as well as the impact of social media on their functioning. Law enforcement and criminal justice agencies may use social media for communication (both internal and external), investigation, and evidence gathering (Denef et al., 2012; Waszkiewicz, 2022). During our study, we have attempted to examine each of these characteristics.

Based on the available data and knowledge about criminal justice practice, we hypothesized that law enforcement agencies would underutilize social media, and when they did use it, it would often be in an ad hoc manner without an organizational framework.

Using a mixed-methods approach and implementing three types of triangulation (Denzin, 2009), we tried to test six main hypotheses:

H1: Law enforcement agencies underutilize social media, and when they do use it, it is primarily to support ongoing investigations.
H2: The use of social media by law enforcement agencies has various effects on their functioning.
H3: Law enforcement personnel have limited knowledge about the use of social media in their work.
H4: Currently, there are no laws, codes of conduct, or best practices regulating the use of social media by law enforcement agencies.
H5: The use of social media by law enforcement agencies will vary depending on the age of the investigators and the popularity of social media in the respective community.
H6: The use of social media by law enforcement agencies depends on the existence of legal acts, codes of conduct, and good practices that regulate its use.

Some of these hypotheses may appear obvious, supported by common knowledge. However, the results of our study paint a more nuanced picture than expected.

DOI: 10.4324/9781032680194-7
This chapter has been made available under a CC-BY-NC 4.0 license.

Only the first part of H1 was confirmed. Law enforcement agents do not use social media very often in their work. This was confirmed by the survey (Chapter 2), and the court files survey revealed the same (Chapter 5). At the same time, selected cases demonstrate that there is potential for using it, and there are skilled law enforcement agents who can take advantage of this in their work (Chapter 6). The percentage of cases in which social media evidence appeared was also significant; it featured in almost a third (32.3%) of the cases examined in Chapter 5. However, it is important to note that the legal qualifications selected have the highest likelihood of containing such materials.

Considering the prevalence of social media in daily life, one might assume that it would be utilized nearly as frequently as traditional forensic techniques such as fingerprinting or DNA analysis. Based on the declared use of social media in Chapter 2 and the results of the quantitative study of court files in Chapter 5, it is evident that the investigative potential of social media is not being fully utilized. Our study indicates that the most extensive use of social media is for public relations and community policing (Chapters 3 and 4), not investigative purposes as we expected.

The study confirmed H2: every Regional Police Department (RPD) in Poland operates its own profile on at least one social media platform (Facebook). Some RPDs operate as many as five such profiles, including on platforms popular among teenagers and young adults, like TikTok. Communication with the general population or regional communities has shifted from traditional media to social media, which allows direct communication, and also constant feedback that shapes future practices.

Securing evidence via social media is becoming a standardized practice. Law enforcement and criminal justice personnel do this on their own, but they also receive such evidence from other parties (Chapters 5 and 6). This is one of the reasons why, in 2022, a new department was established within the Polish police – the Cyberpolice (*Centralne Biuro Zwalczania Cyberprzestępczości*). Its task is not only to fight organized cybercrime but also to help criminal police in their more traditional investigations that involve digital evidence.

The increasing importance of social media in police work is not, however, matched by the knowledge and skills of law enforcement agents. The Cyberpolice is a specialized unit that employs only agents with adequate knowledge and skills. Our surveyed police officers (not from the Cyberpolice) and public prosecutors generally had limited knowledge about social media (Chapter 2). Some of them explicitly confirmed that lack of knowledge and expressed a kind of pride that they never used social media, confirming H3. However, there are some outliers among both groups, with exceptional knowledge and experience in using social media to serve the goals of law enforcement and criminal justice. Outliers are also present among Facebook profile administrators (Chapters 3 and 4). The profiles they manage, such as the Wielkopolska Policja Facebook profile, receive up to four times more likes than the profiles of other RPDs. The rather sparse use of social media in criminal trials, even in cases that could benefit from such evidence (Chapter 5), may be a result of the lack of skills among law enforcement agents.

The results also confirmed H4. There are no specific codes or rules dedicated to the professional use of social media among law enforcement and criminal justice personnel, either to communicate with the general public or to secure evidence. The latter is also true for other types of digital evidence (Lewulis, 2021). One could even question the legitimacy of RPDs maintaining Facebook profiles, since the police could not provide the legal basis for doing so (Waszkiewicz et al., 2021). This is surprising given the popularity and increasing role of social media. The only recommendations in this area pertain to the private use of social media by judges (CEELI, 2019) and prosecutors. The Polish Judges' Rulebook on Professional Ethics recommends that "A judge should exercise restraint in the use of social media" (KRS, 2017). The Principles of Professional Ethics for Polish Prosecutors also recommend prudence and caution when using social media (KRP, 2017).

H5 was partially confirmed. Younger law enforcement agents use social media more often than their older colleagues. This is true for both private and official use (Chapter 3). The most popular social media platforms among law enforcement agents mirror their popularity among the general population.

We could not verify H6, since there are no regulations or even informal good practices for using social media within Polish law enforcement and criminal justice (see H4).

Criminology theories

No single theoretical framework is sufficient to explain the results presented in this book. Therefore, the theories mentioned in the Introduction – Routine Activity Theory, Social Learning Theory, Rational Choice Theory, and Situational Crime Prevention – will be discussed together. This section will also examine some of the theories used by the authors in this book – general strain theory and the self-control theory of crime.

Social media fully meets the conditions of the environment as defined by Routine Activity Theory (Cohen & Felson, 1979). There are potential targets (users) and motivated perpetrators. As with analog environments, a small proportion of perpetrators act in a highly organized manner (Waszkiewicz, 2015). They plan their actions based on a rational assessment of risks and potential benefits, consistent with the tenets of Rational Choice Theory (Nagin & Paternoster, 1993). However, this group did not appear in our court file research (Chapters 5 and 6). They operate in an organized manner, choosing methods that minimize the risk of detection. They remain unidentified, indicating their success. According to the court records survey, most of the prosecuted individuals did not make decisions based on a rational assessment of risks and rewards. They may be considered "amateurs," in contrast to professional perpetrators, who are mostly undetected. Offenders may often succeed because law enforcement agents rarely act as capable guardians. The evidence from interviews with police officers and prosecutors in Chapter 2 indicates that even the most well-prepared law enforcement agents act retroactively. Chapter 6, however, confirms that some law enforcement agents possess forensic knowledge and skills, as shown by both interviewee declarations and qualitative analysis of hate crime proceedings.

The activity of police Facebook profiles fills in some elements of the capable guardian, as discussed in Chapters 3 and 4. However, unorganized activities predominate, as evidenced by a comparison of publication practices. For most RPDs, it is not possible to isolate a strategy. Spokespersons publish most content in an unorganized and, in some cases, haphazard or even chaotic manner. This applies to the content, form, and timing of publications. As with the practices of law enforcement agents, this can be explained by social learning theory (Akers, 2002), although the learning curve is heavily flattened. Both offenders and law enforcement officers have outliers present, and their influence on others is significant. It is likely that many criminals learn new techniques by observing these outliers; the same can be said for law enforcement officers.

Outliers are present both at the individual level, among officers, and at the organizational level, among RPDs. In the case of RPDs, they are also individuals – spokespersons for a particular police unit. Despite the centralized nature of the Polish police, the use of social media has not been unified at any level: communicative, investigative, or evidentiary. To a certain extent, this may be attributed to the absence of formal regulations, collections of best practices, or relevant training. The social media activity of RPDs at the same organizational level varies significantly. These differences were not mitigated by changes during the pandemic (see Chapter 4).

Situational crime prevention theory (Clarke, 1980) can potentially be applied to social media. However, the surveyed law enforcement agencies rarely manipulate situational factors on social media platforms to prevent or deter crime. The educational activities of individual RPDs on their Facebook profiles can be considered as selected elements of situational crime prevention. Law enforcement agencies aim to influence individuals to adopt prosocial behaviors; they also discourage criminal activities by engaging with the community through social media. Wanted perpetrators are detected or uncovered due to their own lack of caution on social media, or that of their loved ones, as in the case of Janusz M., who was wanted by the Polish police for fraud amounting to more than 10 million euros. The police were able to locate him, in part, due to his partner's activity on Instagram (Niebezpiecznik, 2020).

General strain theory (Agnew, 1992) may provide some explanations for the behavior of identified offenders. However, our study did not gather or analyze socioeconomic or psychological data on offenders. Many of the prosecuted offenders confirmed they had acted under the influence of alcohol, emotional tension, or agitation caused by other material watched online; this aligns well with the self-control theory of crime (Gottfredson & Hirschi, 1990). They also expressed regret for their actions (see Chapter 6), although in some cases, individuals may express remorse as a defensive tactic. Self-control theory would account for the existence of two groups of offenders: amateurs who act spontaneously without preparation and often regret their actions and professional outliers who use even unsophisticated techniques to mask their identity.

It appears that the most comprehensive explanation for the use of social media in both perpetrator and law enforcement agent environments is provided by the theory of diffusion of innovations (Rogers, 1962). Although this theory is not specific to criminology, it has been applied in various policing contexts, including SWAT teams, criminal analysis units, and recently body-worn cameras (Wy et al., 2022). In the case of social media, the diffusion of innovations takes longer than one might assume, but this probably does not only apply to the area of criminal justice. Self-conscious innovators, or outliers as we call them, are still few in number, among law enforcement agents, criminals, and the general population. Social media has been incorporated into the lives of billions of people without much reflection. It is now as transparent as other everyday technology solutions.

In 2014, we (Stromczyński & Waszkiewicz, 2014) published the first Polish academic paper on the use of social media by law enforcement agents and agencies. Based on selected examples, we predicted that it would become standard practice in the coming years. We assumed that for individuals born after 1986, social media would be a natural environment and that user awareness would significantly increase. In hindsight, our predictions were partially correct. The results presented in practically every chapter of this book, particularly those concerning court files, confirm this. It is not rocket science to refrain from using one's real personal data and likeness on a social media profile that is used for committing criminal acts, yet most cases involving evidence from social media contained the perpetrator's real personal information. It is difficult to believe that all these perpetrators acted under the influence of intoxicants.

The diffusion of innovations in the social media sphere has limitations even among those who have been using it regularly for years. In late 2023, a Polish celebrity influencer and the leader of the winning opposition coalition inadvertently disclosed payment card numbers on their social media profiles (Niebezpiecznik, 2023). They did not commit any criminal acts; the issue is about being aware of what information one shares with other users on social media – or the lack of such awareness.

Policy implications: education first

The book's results have policy implications. The necessity for education on social media is of utmost importance. The underutilization of social media is mainly due to a lack of knowledge and skills. Law enforcement agents on the front line do not need to know the technical details of securing digital evidence; however, they should understand its importance at the investigative and evidentiary level. It is insufficient to assume that because young people use these tools regularly, they will be knowledgeable about them. The results indicate a deficiency in relevant training and underutilization of the tools. Whatever the branding and functionality of future social media platforms, they will likely continue to be used even more frequently than at present. To achieve the goals of law enforcement agencies more effectively, training should also be extended to those who manage social media profiles in RPDs and other units at different levels.

No new legislation is necessary specifically for the use of social media by law enforcement or criminal justice more broadly. Social media evidence shares the characteristics of digital evidence (Lewulis, 2021). If it is regulated by existing laws (which is not the case in Poland), then no legislative action is required. However, the use of social media by law enforcement agencies could be improved through the implementation of clear internal guidelines or best practices, including information on how to obtain and preserve social media material for investigative and evidentiary purposes. It should also cover what to do when a victim or witness provides such materials themselves, as is becoming more common. Our results show that law enforcement agents have varying practices when it comes to securing and presenting social media evidence for litigation, based solely on their personal judgment. Such guidelines should also address the need for tailored communication for those who administer profiles or communicate with the general public. Communication activities should not, however, be modeled on influencers; law enforcement has different goals.

The communication, investigative, and evidentiary functions of social media use have been separated in this section; each type requires different preparations for law enforcement agents. When used in combination, they allow for the full potential of social media to be realized – potential that was already highlighted a decade ago in the first international study of law enforcement agents (Denef et al., 2012). It is surprising that a centralized law enforcement model lacks such practices.

Without a large-scale implementation of training and the parallel development of consistent guidelines, criminal justice and law enforcement will continue their current practice of inconsistent solutions. At present, good practices are disseminated slowly through observation of outliers, while some law enforcement agents fear using this tool. This fear is particularly prevalent among older law enforcement agents who hold higher positions in the hierarchical structure of law enforcement. Recommendations on ethics that require prudence and caution when using social media, though accurate in themselves, may exacerbate fears and lead to a decision not to use it at all.

According to the Red Queen theory, law enforcement must constantly adapt to keep up with changes in its retroactive design (Waszkiewicz, 2015). It seems that in recent years, the criminal justice system in Poland has made a sham of adapting to social media. We believe that the limited exploitation of this by criminals can be attributed to the prevalence of amateur laggards among perpetrators. Global and regional crises, such as the COVID-19 pandemic and the war in Ukraine, may have contributed to the failure to take this issue seriously. However, there will never be a better time for change that goes beyond the introduction of yet another legal provision.

References

Agnew, R. (1992). Foundation for a general strain theory of crime and delinquency. *Criminology*, *30*(1), 47–88. https://doi.org/10.1111/j.1745-9125.1992.tb01093.x

Akers, R. L. (2002). A social learning theory of crime. In C. Suzett (Ed.), *Criminological theories: Bridging the past to the future*, (pp. 135–143). SAGE. ISBN: 9780761925033

CEELI. (2019). *Practical guidelines on use of social media by judges*. https://ceeliinstitute.org/resource/practical-guidelines-on-use-of-social-media-by-judges

Clarke, R. V. (1980). Situational crime prevention: Theory and practice. *The British Journal of Criminology*, *20*(20), 136–147. https://doi.org/10.1093/oxfordjournals.bjc.a047153

Cohen, L. E., & Felson, M. (1979). Social change and crime rate trends: A routine activity approach. *American Sociological Review*, *44*(4), 588. https://doi.org/10.2307/2094589

Denef, S., Kaptein, N., Bayerl, S., & Ramirez, L. (2012). *Best practice in police social media adaptation*. http://hdl.handle.net/1765/40562

Denzin, N. K. (2009). The elephant in the living room: Or extending the conversation about the politics of evidence. *Qualitative research*, *9*(2), 139–160.

Gottfredson, M. R., & Hirschi, T. (1990). *A general theory of crime*. Stanford University Press. ISBN: 9780804717748

Lewulis, P. (2021). *Dowody cyfrowe – teoria i praktyka kryminalistyczna w polskim postępowaniu karnym*. University of Warsaw Press. https://doi.org/10.31338/uw.9788323548027

Nagin, D. S., & Paternoster, R. (1993). Enduring individual differences and rational choice theories of crime. *Law and Society Review*, *27*(2), 467–496. https://doi.org/10.2307/3054102

Niebezpiecznik. (2020). Uszczuplił skarb państwa o 50 mln zł. Wpadł z powodu fotek partnerki w social mediach, https://niebezpiecznik.pl/post/partnerka-poszukiwanego-janusza-m-wrzucala-fotki-do-social-mediow-zgadnij-co-sie-stalo/

Niebezpiecznik. (2023). *Karta płatnicza Donalda Tuska widoczna na filmiku, który wrzucił do sieci*. https://niebezpiecznik.pl/post/donald-tusk-karta-platnicza/

Rogers, E. M. (1962). *Diffusion of innovations*. Free Press of Glencoe.

Stromczyński, B., & Waszkiewicz, P. (2014). Biały wywiad w praktyce pracy organów ścigania na przykładzie wykorzystania serwisów społecznościowych. *Prokuratura i Prawo*, *5*, 146–170.

Uchwała nr 15/17 Krajowej Rady Sądownictwa z dnia 11 stycznia 2017 r.

Waszkiewicz, P. (2015). *Traktat o dobrej prewencji kryminalnej*. Towarzystwo Inicjatyw Prawnych i Kryminalistycznych Paragraf 22. ISBN: 978-83-943011-0-1

Waszkiewicz, P. (Ed.). (2022). *Media społecznościowe w postępowaniu karnym*. Wydawnictwo INP PAN. https://doi.org/10.5281/zenodo.6497415

Waszkiewicz, P., Tomaszewska-Michalak, M., Stromczyński, B., & Rabczuk, S. (2021). Nie pytają Cię o imię, walczą z ostrym cieniem mgły. Podstawy prawne wykorzystania mediów społecznościowych przez polskie organy władzy publicznej na przykładzie Policji, *Studia Iuridica*, *89*, 386–408. https://doi.org/10.31338/2544-3135.si.2022-89.20

Wy, G. C., Gaub, J. E., & Koen, M. C. (2022). The impacts of body-worn cameras: An examination of police specialty unit perceptions through diffusion of innovations. *American Journal of Criminal Justice*, *47*(2), 224–245. https://doi.org/10.1007/s12103-021-09624-x

Załącznik do uchwały Krajowej Rady Prokuratorów Przy Prokuratorze Generalnym z dnia 12 grudnia 2017 r. Zbiór Zasad Etyki Zawodowej Prokuratorów.

Index

Note: Page numbers in *italics* indicates figures and page numbers in **bold** indicates tables.

For Product Safety Concerns and Information please contact our EU representative GPSR@taylorandfrancis.com
Taylor & Francis Verlag GmbH, Kaufingerstraße 24, 80331 München, Germany

www.ingramcontent.com/pod-product-compliance
Ingram Content Group UK Ltd.
Pitfield, Milton Keynes, MK11 3LW, UK
UKHW022157190926
475702UK00003B/74
9781032680187